C. DAVID MEAD

Professor of English, Michigan State University

ADVISORY EDITOR TO DODD, MEAD & COMPANY

WORD, SELF, REALITY:

THE RHETORIC OF IMAGINATION

WORD, SELF, REALITY

The Rhetoric of Imagination

JAMES E. MILLER, JR.

The University of Chicago

Dodd, Mead & Company

NEW YORK   1973   TORONTO

ACKNOWLEDGMENTS

Acknowledgment is made to the following publishers for permission to use excerpts from the works cited.

ATHENEUM PUBLISHERS, INC.: From *The Firmament of Time* by Loren Eiseley. Copyright © 1960 by Loren Eiseley; copyright © 1960 by the Trustees of the University of Pennsylvania. Reprinted by permission of Atheneum Publishers.

GEORGE BRAZILLER, INC.: From *Sign, Image, Symbol,* Vision + Value Series, Gyorgy Kepes, ed. Copyright © by George Braziller, Inc.

NORMAN O. BROWN: From "Apocalypse: The Mystery in the Life of the Mind" by Norman O. Brown. Copyright © 1961 by Minneapolis Star and Tribune Co., Inc. Reprinted from the May, 1961 issue of *Harper's Magazine* by permission of the author.

JONATHAN CAPE LTD: From *Death in the Afternoon* by Ernest Hemingway. Reprinted by permission of the Executors of the Ernest Hemingway Estate and Jonathan Cape Ltd.

CHARING CROSS MUSIC, INC.: From "The Sound of Silence." © 1964 Paul Simon. Reprinted by permission of Charing Cross Music, Inc.

CITY LIGHTS BOOKS.: From "Sunflower Sutra" by Allen Ginsberg. Copyright © 1956, 1959 by Allen Ginsberg. Reprinted by permission of City Lights Books.

CONTINENTAL TOTAL MEDIA PROJECT, INC.: From "Suzanne" by Leonard Cohen. Copyright 1966. Reprinted by permission of Continental Total Media Project, Inc.

DEVON MUSIC, INC.: "My Generation" by Peter Townshend. © copyright 1965 Fabulous Music, Ltd., London, England. Tro-Devon Music, Inc., New York, controls all publication rights for the U.S.A. and Canada. Reprinted by permission.

ANDRE DEUTSCH, LTD.: From *Advertisements for Myself* by Norman Mailer. Reprinted by permission.

DOUBLEDAY & COMPANY, INC.: From *Culture and Commitment* by Margaret Mead. Copyright © 1970 by Margaret Mead. / From *An Introduction to Haiku* by Harold G. Henderson. Copyright © by Harold G. Henderson. / From *Man and His Symbols* by Carl G. Jung. Copyright ©

THE NEW YORK REVIEW OF BOOKS: From *Teaching the "Unteachable"* by Herbert R. Kohl. Copyright 1967 by Herbert R. Kohl. Reprinted with permission of *The New York Review of Books.*

NORTHERN SONGS LIMITED: From "Strawberry Fields Forever." Words and music by John Lennon and Paul McCartney. Copyright 1967 Northern Songs Ltd. Reprinted by permission.

PETER OWEN LTD.: From *Siddhartha* by Hermann Hesse, translated by Hilda Rosner. Reprinted by permission.

PENGUIN BOOKS LTD.: From *The Politics of Experience* by R. D. Laing. Copyright © 1967 by R. D. Laing. Reprinted by permission of Penguin Books Ltd.

LAURENCE POLLINGER LIMITED: From *The Collected Earlier Poems* by William Carlos Williams ("The Red Wheelbarrow"). Published by MacGibbon & Kee Ltd. Reprinted by permission of Laurence Pollinger Limited.

G. P. PUTNAM'S SONS: From *Advertisements for Myself* by Norman Mailer. Copyright © 1959 by Norman Mailer. Reprinted by permission of G. P. Putnam's Sons.

RANDOM HOUSE, INC.–ALFRED A. KNOPF, INC.: From *The Invisible Man* by Ralph Ellison. Copyright 1952 by Ralph Ellison. / From *Down These Mean Streets* by Piri Thomas. Copyright © 1967 by Piri Thomas. / From *The Necessary Angel* by Wallace Stevens. Copyright 1951 by Wallace Stevens. / From the following works of William Faulkner: *The Sound and the Fury,* copyright 1929 by William Faulkner, renewed 1957; *Absolam, Absolam,* copyright 1936 by William Faulkner and renewed 1964 by Estelle Faulkner and Jill Faulkner Summers; *Faulkner at West Point,* copyright © 1964 by Random House, Inc.; *Essays and Speeches,* copyright © 1965 by Random House, Inc. / All reprinted by permission of Random House, Inc.–Alfred A. Knopf, Inc.

RIDER & COMPANY: *Essays in Zen Buddhism,* First Series, by D. T. Suzuki. Reprinted by permission.

ROUTLEDGE & KEGAN PAUL LTD: From *Tractatus Logico-Philosophicus* by Ludwig Wittgenstein. Reprinted by permission.

CHARLES SCRIBNER'S SONS: From *Death in the Afternoon* by Ernest Hemingway. Reprinted by permission.

MARTIN SECKER & WARBURG LIMITED: From *Writers At Work:* The Paris Review Interviews. Reprinted by permission.

STUDIO VISTA PUBLISHERS: From *Sign, Image, Symbol,* edited by Gyorgy Kepes. Reprinted by permission.

CHARLES E. TUTTLE PUBLISHING CO., INC.: From *Zen Flesh, Zen Bones* by Paul Reps. Reprinted by permission.

UNIVERSITY OF CALIFORNIA PRESS: From *Culture, Language and Personality* by Edward Sapir, Selected Essays edited by David G. Mandelbaum, 1949. Reprinted by permission.

VANGUARD PRESS, INC.: From *The Victim* by Saul Bellow. Reprinted by permission.

THE VIKING PRESS, INC.: From *Writers at Work:* The Paris Review Interviews, Second Series. Copyright © 1963 by The Paris Review, Inc. All rights reserved. / From *Writers at Work:* The Paris Review Interviews edited by Malcolm Cowley. Copyright © 1957, 1958 by the Paris Review, Inc. / All reprinted by permission of the Viking Press, Inc.

PREFATORY NOTE

Word, Self, Reality: The Rhetoric of Imagination has been written in a spirit of intellectual centrifugality; with the aim of spinning the reader, again and again, out of his own orbit into other orbits—intellectual, imaginative, linguistic—for deeper exploration and personal discovery. But it has been written, too, to exert some alternating centripetal force—pulling the reader back from his exploratory journeys, and preparing him for further points of departure, more distant flights.

Although the book is written from an individual point of view, it does not represent the isolated thought of one man, but the collected thoughts of many men—experimenters and thinkers in many different activities. It has been, in fact, designed as a "collaboration," with each of its parts preceded by and interspersed with quotations that have been carefully selected to suggest a frame of reference for what is being proposed or affirmed. These quotations are sometimes left entirely on their own, not even mentioned in the main text. The assumption is that they will quietly provide resonance for the ideas under discussion; that they will point in unexplored directions; that they will entice the reader into depths and complexities beyond the limits dealt with in the book.

Word, Self, Reality has been designed to inform and inspire the beginning writer as well as challenge the more advanced. Its main ideas should prove accessible and valuable to both. A teacher's manual to help in adapting the book to a variety of levels is available to teachers only from the publisher.

The quotations are drawn from a variety of specialists and generalists and writers in a variety of fields—from anthropologists, psychologists, philosophers, semanticists, linguists, poets, novelists, essayists, cultural analysts, scientists, and social scientists.

This breadth is the result of a deliberate effort to bring to bear some of the best thought of these disparate areas on the problems of writing. Students of English have for too long studied language and composition in isolation from the important discoveries of the spoken and written language by other disciplines. A major aim of this book is to point up the relevance to writing of these several fields.

Among the writers quoted in the book are the following (passages are always documented to make further investigations easy: consult the footnotes, the bibliography, or the index at the end of the book): Norman O. Brown, Truman Capote, Rudolph Carnap, Lewis Carroll, Ernst Cassirer, Noam Chomsky, Leonard Cohen, René Dubos, T. S. Eliot, Ralph Waldo Emerson, William Faulkner, Walker Gibson, S. Giedion, Lorraine Hansberry, Ernest Hemingway, Hermann Hesse, Henry James, William James, Otto Jespersen, LeRoi Jones, Carl G. Jung, Clyde Kluckhohn, R. D. Laing, Susanne K. Langer, John Lennon, Marshall McLuhan, Norman Mailer, Abraham H. Maslow, Margaret Mead, H. L. Mencken, Lewis Mumford, Frank O'Connor, Walter J. Ong, J. Robert Oppenheimer, Jean Piaget, Edward Sapir, Georges Simenon, Paul Simon, Susan Sontag, Wilhelm Stekel, Wallace Stevens, William Styron, D. T. Suzuki, Piri Thomas, Peter Townshend, Kurt Vonnegut, Jr., L. S. Vygotsky, Alfred North Whitehead, Walt Whitman, William Carlos Williams, Ludwig Wittgenstein, Virginia Woolf.

Other writers (in addition to many of the above), whose quoted passages bear more directly on the text or the exercises, are: John Barth, Matsuo Bashō, Saul Bellow, William Blake, Martin Buber, Lord Byron, Eldridge Cleaver, E. E. Cummings, Emily Dickinson, Ralph Ellison, Loren Eiseley, Allen Ginsberg, Dag Hammarskjöld, Joseph Heller, James Joyce, Malcolm X, A. M. Quinton, Theodore Roszak, Gertrude Stein, Henry David Thoreau, Henry Vaughan.

These lists almost exhaust the encounters in the book, but not quite. There are quotations culled from *The Upanishads, Current Research on Dreams, 101 Zen Stories,* and other exotic (as well as mundane) places—but these are enough to suggest something of the reach of the book.

It is impossible to name all the people who have helped to shape my thinking on language and composition. But I must mention a key experience which affected me deeply: The Anglo-American conference on the teaching of English, held at Dartmouth College in the summer of 1966. Participation in the debates and discussions with my American and British colleagues brought new dimensions to my thinking about the role of creativity in English teaching and learning. My views, however, are my own, and have been arrived at only after some considerable rethinking of some wide-spread assumptions in the teaching of writing. I want to thank a number of people for reading and commenting on the manuscript in its earlier stages: Martha Cox, Carol Hunter, Stephen Judy, and David Mead. And a number of people at Dodd, Mead have been more helpful than they know: William Oman in challenging me to write the book in the first place; Virginia Hans in making substantial and valuable suggestions as the manuscript went through revision; and Genia Graves in moving the book gently through the details of printing and publication.

J. E. M., JR.

CONTENTS

WORD, SELF, REALITY:

THE RHETORIC OF IMAGINATION

IMAGINATION AND WRITING

The imagination is the power of the mind over the possibilities of things. . . . We cannot look at the past or the future except by means of the imagination. . . . [The imagination] enables us to live our own lives. We have it because we do not have enough without it. . . . The imagination is the power that enables us to perceive the normal in the abnormal, the opposite of chaos in chaos. . . . The truth seems to be that we live in concepts of the imagination before the reason has established them. If this is true, then reason is simply the methodizer of the imagination. It may be that the imagination is a miracle of logic and that its exquisite divinations are calculations beyond analysis, as the conclusions of the reason are calculations wholly within analysis. If so, one understands perfectly that "in the service of love and imagination nothing can be too lavish, too sublime or too festive."

> Wallace Stevens, "Imagination as Value,"
> *The Necessary Angel,* 1951.

Unconscious thinking, perceiving, or communication is archaic (in Jung's sense), mythological, poetic, metaphorical, preverbal, often concrete rather than conceptualized. It is characteristic of our night and day dreams, of our imagination, of revery, of an essential aspect of all art, of the first stages of creative production, of free association, etc. It is generally stigmatized by most well-adjusted, sane, sober adults in the West as childish, crazy, senseless, wild. It is thus threatening to their adult adjustment to the outer world, regarded as incompatible with it and therefore often repudiated. This means it cannot be communicated with, and cannot be used.

> Abraham H. Maslow, "Isomorphic Interrelationships
> Between Knower and Known," *Sign, Image, Symbol,* 1966.

1

This book has been written in the belief that the best approach to writing does not consist of a series of don'ts, a list of restraints and restrictions. Such series and lists tend to trivialize language and to diminish its potential in human creativity. Language is too vital in our lives and too important in our fate to reduce it to a matter of "good grammar" or refined propriety. This is not a book, then, about when to use *who* or *whom,* or when you might get by with saying *ain't,* or when to use *like* and when to use *as.* Such matters have nothing to do with the vitality of language and the limitless possibilities of writing.

Nor is this a book about externals of form—sentences, paragraphs, essays; exposition, narration, description, argumentation; fiction, poetry, drama. All of us have rudimentary notions of these elements or forms. And laboring over elaborate definitions of them and distinctions among them will contribute little to our writing: the truth is that memorizing definitions has nothing to do with our ability to write particular forms. Moreover, such definitions are usually arbitrary and often artificial since pure form is a myth. If we look at any piece of writing, we find narration mixed up with exposition, argument creeping into description, fiction filtering through poetry, and poetry encroaching on drama. Sometimes fixed and rigid notions about form will cause one to distort reality, demanding purity where there is only alloy. It is better to remain flexible, and to take writing as we find it, not as we might wish it to follow from pat and tidy definitions.

This book, furthermore, does not attempt to explain writing as a matter of learning how to develop paragraphs and organize essays. Comparison and contrast, definition, accumulation of detail—these also become all mixed up in the reality of writing. There is little to be gained by concentrating attention on them for prolonged periods, or on the making of or abiding by outlines. When a child starts school, he is already speaking sentences (psycho-linguists tell us that he is internally programmed for use of the language) and to pretend to teach him to speak sentences is a hoax. When you reach this book, too, you are already thoroughly immersed in the written language and, in some sense, programmed for its use. Emphasis on the externals of writing will be of little value.

What this book does attempt to do is to restore awareness of the mystery of language and respect for its ways and its possibilities. Some basic assumptions run through the book. The first of these is that writing must be motivated, and that the best writing is deeply motivated; therefore, any attempt to induce writing must begin by tapping feelings—desire, pain, ambition, curiosity, and many more. A second assumption is that once the motivation is stimulated, it will in turn tap language resources dammed up inside every human being: language will rush forth when the need and desire are genuine. A third assumption running through the book is that language must serve the individual, in a fundamental way, in the exploration and discovery of himself and his world; and it must also serve the individual by relating and connecting him to others, in dialogue, discussion, and communication. A fourth and important assumption is that a moratorium should be declared on propriety in language. The desire for "correctness" (or, in the popular idiom, "good grammar") should spring from within, and not be imposed from without; the desire will come when the writer strongly wants a hearing from those demanding such propriety.

The mystery of language is, in large part, the mystery of the processes of the imagination; indeed, language and imagination are so closely intertwined that it would be impossible to untangle them. Probably there is no use of language that does not involve some part of the imagination. And, conversely, the imagination no doubt finds some of its finest manifestations in language. For too long the assumption has been made that language used by an individual originates in the orderly processes of his rational mind, in his reason, in his faculty of systematic logic. Instruction in language-use has therefore been largely aimed at this logical faculty, in the belief that the teaching of orderly processes will result in good writing. The result, though, has too often been not good writing but dead writing, obedient to all the inhibitions and restraints drilled into the reason, but generally dehumanized and unreadable.

The power which makes all things new is magic. What our time needs is mystery: what our time needs is magic. Who would not say that only a miracle can save us?
> Norman O. Brown, "Apocalypse: The Place of
> Mystery in the Life of the Mind,"
> *Harper's Magazine*, May 1961.

For the truth seems to be (the truth accepted by this book, anyway) that language-use owes more to the imaginative faculty of the mind than to the logical. This truth appears demonstrable in all the language-use around us every day, verbal and written, and even in those pieces of writing that purport to be absolutely "logical" (but so often fail to persuade their readers). The imagination feeds the roots of any writing that remains readable, and flashes forth from the finished page for any reader to note. The imaginative sources of language may be discovered by introspection, by an honest examination of the way we speak and write the language. We do not labor with logic or agonize in reason before we state our serious opinion. Beneath whatever logic and reason we tentatively consult, lie feelings and emotions that have bent us in a particular direction; and lurking everywhere is the imagination which, even on the most complicated subject, provides us with humor and wit and depth.

One apostle and poet of the imagination, Wallace Stevens, has pointed out the simple fact that "We cannot look at the past or the future except by means of the imagination." To liberate ourselves from *this* moment in time and the immediate range of vision in *this* place, we must use the imagination. Simple reflection should bring home to us what a powerful liberating force the imagination is, and how essential it is to language and particularly to writing—which is most often concerned with matters beyond this fleeting moment and this narrow stretch of earth in view. Without the imagination we would be imprisoned in time and space, and would be without language in the sense that we know it. With imagination we are enabled, through language, to free ourselves for explorations and discoveries that give meaning to ourselves and our society.

The process of the imagination, as it embraces language, remains shrouded in the mystery of the working of the human mind. Many great creative minds have testified to this mystery, and have expressed their awe of it. Henry James, in describing the way an idea for a story came to him, says that all of a sudden he *saw* the figures of his story; and after giving an account of this sudden possession of his material, he says: ". . . it will commend itself, I feel, to all imaginative and projective persons who have had—and what imaginative and projective person hasn't?—any like experience of the suddenly-determined *absolute* of perception. The whole cluster of items forming the image is on these occasions born at once; the parts are not pieced together, they conspire and interdepend; but what it really comes to, no doubt, is that at a simple touch an old latent and dormant impression, a buried germ, implanted by experience and then forgotten, flashes to the surface as a fish, with a single 'squirm,' rises to the baited hook, and there meets instantly the vivifying ray."[1] Few of us

1. Henry James, *The Art of the Novel* (New York: Charles Scribner's Sons, 1934), p. 151.

have written novels, or even attempted it, but all of us have experienced moments of illumination or insight or awareness such as that James describes. The process of the imagination, with modifications and variations and transformations, is a part, and probably the most important part, of any process of writing—but a part that has been virtually ignored by all the handbooks on composition.

If we may extend James's metaphor, we might say that the use of language, particularly in writing, involves a fishing in deep waters. We must constantly be on the lookout for what might rise to the baited hook, what might at any moment flash to the surface and present itself to our view. If when that moment comes we are bogged down in the quicksands of logic and reason, we might let the fish of the imagination get away. This metaphor perhaps distorts the reality of writing somewhat, but not as much as descriptions which make it entirely a rational and logical act. The chapters of this book have been written to get as close to the reality of language-use and of writing as it is possible to get. They are presented not with the intent of revealing a series of absolute truths, but of inspiring thought, reaction, and imaginative response, and of provoking a desire to write and explore.

A Preliminary Question—*Why write?*

At the beginning of any book on writing, the question should be posed, Why write? There was a time, in prehistory, when man did not write. There are primitive tribes now in existence whose sophisticated languages (linguists tell us that no languages are primitive) remain entirely oral.

But in this bewildering technological, electronic culture, reading and writing are matters of survival. What one becomes will largely depend on mastery of these interrelated arts. Not simply what one becomes in the occupational or professional sense, but what one becomes as an individual human being—a person of surfaces or depths, of density or awareness. The technitronic, computerized culture, with all its alleged blessings, brings with it not only a crisis in jobs and professions, but also a crisis (perhaps the more personally agonizing) in *being human* for the individual *human being*.

No abstract generalization will be so persuasive as an individual case. Eldridge Cleaver, in *Soul on Ice*, answered the question, Why write? He explained in his essay "On Becoming" that it was simply a matter of—salvation: "That is why I started to write. To save myself. I realized that no one would save me but myself. The prison authorities were both uninterested and unable to help me. I had to seek out the truth and unravel the snarled web of my motivations. I had to find out who I am and what I want to be, what type of man I should be, and what I could do to become the best of which I was capable."[2] It is doubtful that any of us could formulate a better reason for writing—*to seek out the truth and unravel the snarled web of our motivations*. That is perhaps enough. But if we found out who we are or what we might become—in the genuine sense of *become*—then what more important service can we perform for ourselves than to write; to write, that is, not to get a grade or pass a course, but to sound the depths, to explore, to discover; to save our floundering *selves*.

2. Eldridge Cleaver, "On Becoming," *Soul on Ice* (New York: McGraw-Hill Co., 1968; rpt. Dell Publishing Co., 1968), p. 15.

> **They [my writings] are things I wrote because to maintain myself in a world much of which I didn't love I had to fight to keep myself as I wanted to be.**
> William Carlos Williams,
> *Selected Letters*
> (letter to his son, 1942).

PART ONE

WORDS IN THE WORLD

The first three chapters of this book, roughly one-half of the work, form a sequence emphasizing the ways—mysterious and mundane—that language interpenetrates our every experience and affects and shapes our lives. This part of the book has been designed to develop an alertness to the ubiquity of language in the world, an awareness of the complexity of words in the processes of thinking and feeling, and a sensitivity to the ambiguity of words in the shifting realms of meaning. Although the thrust is theoretical, the intent of this part is practical: to provoke you into seeing, experiencing, and using what has probably become, through familiarity, unnoticed or invisible—*words in the world*.

I. LANGUAGE AS CREATION

1. The Linguistic Environment

And in the naked light I saw
Ten thousand people maybe more,
People talking without speaking,
People hearing without listening,
People writing songs that voices never share
And no one dares disturb the sound of silence.
  Paul Simon, "The Sound of Silence," 1964.

... if the function of language were merely to "communicate," the phenomenon of verbalism would hardly admit of explanation. How could words, confined as they are by usage to certain precise meanings (precise, because their object is to be understood), eventually come to veil the confusion of thought, even to create obscurity by the multiplication of verbal entities, and actually to prevent thought from being communicable? This is not the place to raise the vexed question of the relation between thought and language, but we may note in passing that the very existence of such questions shows how complex are the functions of language, and how futile the attempt to reduce them all to one—that of communicating thought.
  Jean Piaget, *The Language and Thought of the Child,* 1930.

It is best at the outset of another attempt at mastering the art of writing to pause and consider in some depth the nature of the material you are asked to use: language. What is language? The answer to that question might well seal up the flow forever, or fling back the floodgates and let it out in full stream. . . .

It must be candidly admitted that there is no universally accepted definition of language. The linguistic scientist sees language as an immensely fascinating grammatical structure which may be observed, examined, and analyzed in a number of ways. A boy in the seventh grade, on the other hand, sees language as "a bunch of rules"—and he pronounces this definition with a grimace on his face and suspicion in his heart.

There are books that will tell you that language is a means for communication of ideas, a system of symbols used to convey thought. The problem with these and other such definitions is that they mistake a part for the whole. They are like the definitions of man supplied by a professor of anatomy: man is made up of a complex set of interrelated muscles, organs, and bones which serve to enable him to grow and reproduce himself. We might well ask, Is that all? What has happened to the living, breathing creature with a soul—you or me?

The best way to shake these limited definitions out of our minds is to stand back deliberately from the rush of experience and watch the way language permeates all life. We notice, of course, that we use language to embody experiences as we tell tales and, in turn, listen to stories about "what happened." But we notice too, that language not only embodies experience, but actually exists as a part of experience. To say something, to hear something said—these are acts of behavior, component parts of a situation, an incident, a full-scale happening—a story in all of its narrative and emotional complexity.

But language is still more than the means for embodying and engaging in experience. We live, literally, *in* and *by* and *with*

I. LANGUAGE AS CREATION

language. We wake to be bombarded with radio or television news or chatter, muttering back our feelings of outrage or gratitude as we busy ourselves preparing our bodies and faces for another day of encounter with the world—through language. As we drink our orange juice we scan the newspaper and keep up a running stream of linguistic response—*oh, the neighbor's boy's in an automobile wreck, the peace negotiations are getting nowhere oh boy what a world, the president is going to veto a money bill but the Congress will probably override the veto, the stockmarket fell again I wonder how that affects my shrinking funds, oh there was a murder just a few blocks from the house, I wonder. . . .* The stream of private language will be occasionally broken by utterances aloud, to a companion or acquaintance. And as the day progresses, and the night-stiffness wears off the tongue, it will loosen and move readily through the motions of speech, sounding out the world, reaching out to a friend, holding off a foe at arm's length, tying up a deal with considerable craft, cajoling a girlfriend, conveying feelings, concealing emotions, exploring meaning, trying out ideas, concealing intentions, and on and on and on, endlessly wagging, pouring out at intervals streams of sound that move through and shape the world, hold it off and let it in, try it out, turn it up, down, or off.

This linguistic encounter with the world is by no means one-way. Accompanying the outflow, frequently motivating and modulating it, is the constant inflow—the stream of language from the outside to the inside—much of it through the ear, but as much or more through the eye, as we listen and read our way through life. As we sit in a restaurant over coffee, engaged with friends in a discussion of politics or religion or sex, we hear a radio in the corner blaring the latest casualty figures in the most recent war; we glance at the headlines on a newspaper in the lap of a friend; we glimpse the label on a ketchup bottle on the table; we note on the back of a book of matches the warning to get a medical

The dictionaries still say that "language is a device for communicating ideas." The semanticists and the anthropologists agree that this is a tiny, specialized function of speech. Mainly, language is an instrument for action. The meaning of a word or phrase is not its dictionary equivalent but the difference its utterance brings about in a situation. We use words to comfort and cajole ourselves in fantasy and daydream, to let off steam, to goad ourselves into one type of activity and to deny ourselves another. We use words to promote our own purposes in dealing with others. We build up verbal pictures of ourselves and our motives. We coax, wheedle, protest, invite, and threaten. Even the most intellectual of intellectuals employs only a minute fraction of his total utterance in symbolizing and communicating ideas that are divorced from emotion and action. The primary social value of speech lies in getting individuals to work more effectively together and in easing social tensions. Very often what is said matters much less than that something is said.

Clyde Kluckhohn, "The Gift of Tongues," *Mirror for Man*, 1949.

checkup for lung cancer; we see through the window a sign saying STOP; we read a giant billboard down the street promoting a brand of cigarettes with a foolproof filter; we hear stray words arise from the buzz of conversation throughout the restaurant; we tune in briefly to a whispered boy-girl quarrel at a nearby table; we flip through a paperback copy of the Bhagavad Gita that we bought on impulse at the newsstand.

We live surrounded by language as by air, taking it in and releasing it as naturally as we inhale and exhale. We are bombarded on every side, assaulted at every hour, by language demanding, commanding attention; and we are forced to pick and choose, to tune in or tune out, to see and read or turn and depart, to say yes or no or maybe, to argue or agree or remain suspended

I. LANGUAGE AS CREATION

in doubt. We thread our way through the maze of many tongues; we make money or we make love, we encounter the world, which shapes us as we shape it, we know life as it comes to know us— all through words, words, words.

Words do not simply accompany experience; more frequently they *are* the experience, or are its primary content. We live surrounded by language, inside and outside us. It can strangle and suffocate us, or it can connect and link, strengthen and renew us. Language, then, is far more than mere communication; it is indeed a kind of creation. With it we make our world and ourselves. Through our daily linguistic encounter with the world, we proclaim our identities, shape our lives, and (in some small or big way) leave our impress on the world.

Ideas and Experiments

1. Keep a running account for one day of your use of and encounter with language. Calculate how much time was spent in

> ... the purely communicative aspect of language has been exaggerated. It is best to admit that language is primarily a vocal actualization of the tendency to see realities symbolically, that it is precisely this quality which renders it a fit instrument for communication and that it is in the actual give and take of social intercourse that it has been complicated and refined into the form in which it is known today.
>
> Edward Sapir, "Language," 1933

various categories that you identify—in communicating ideas, in expressing emotions, in exploring relationships, in absorbing facts, etc.

2. Concentrate on a single episode during the day, a coffee break, a luncheon, a bull session: describe the variety of linguistic elements that entered into the occasion, those that were intentional as well as those that were accidental. Describe and attempt to account for the course of talk or conversation, how it moved from topic to topic and why.

3. Examine an episode or a series of related episodes in your daily life of semiaccidental encounters and explore how the language-content shaped the events. Consider how the events would have been changed by different linguistic responses on your part.

4. In what way do you see your use of language as an extension of yourself? Are you aware enough of your own language to speculate how your linguistic identity appears to others? Present your own linguistic portrait, or do a brief study of someone else you know who has a strong linguistic identity.

Further Points of Departure

1. Write a letter to yourself from your father (or mother) giving you advice on how to get along in an uncertain, dangerous, and cruel world, with particular emphasis on the various kinds of treacherous people you will meet (or are meeting).

2. Write a letter from yourself to your father (or mother) explaining how all the advice he has given you has not (or has) prepared you for the world you have met outside the home he provided.

2. Interior Language

Until quite lately the unit of mental life which figured most was the single "idea," supposed to be a definitely outlined thing. But at present psychologists are tending, first, to admit that the actual unit is more probably the total mental state, the entire wave of consciousness or field of objects present to the thought at any time; and, second, to see that it is impossible to outline this wave, this field, with any definiteness.

As our mental fields succeed one another, each has its centre of interest, around which the objects of which we are less and less attentively conscious fade to a margin so faint that its limits are unassignable. Some fields are narrow fields and some are wide fields. Usually when we have a wide field we rejoice, for we then see masses of truth together, and often get glimpses of relations which we divine rather than see, for they shoot beyond the field into still remoter regions of objectivity, regions which we seem rather to be about to perceive than to perceive actually.

. . . but . . . there is not only the consciousness of the ordinary field, with its usual centre and margin, but an addition thereto in the shape of a set of memories, thoughts, and feelings which are extramarginal and outside of the primary consciousness altogether, but yet must be classed as conscious facts of some sort, able to reveal their presence by unmistakable signs.

William James, *The Varieties of Religious Experience*, 1902.

If we live daily in an external chaos of language which forces us to select and arrange, to place in context and put in order, we also feel something of the chaos of language churning inside us, welling up from depths, darting in from the dim sidelines, appearing and disappearing with a bewildering and uncontrollable rapidity. As we must come to terms with the language chaos without, so we must adjust to the chaos of language within. But we can do more than adjust. We can look upon the ceaseless flow of language within us as one of our most precious resources. We can view it as a great flood rolling rapidly along, floating on and in its waters the treasures of the world, to be snatched out and put to creative use.

All of us live rich inner linguistic lives, lives fantastically full of imaginative leaps and spurts; of language tangles that mass suddenly like barbed wire balls and barriers and dissolve as suddenly by a "poof" of fragmentary fantasy; of language explanations that build laboriously on successive solid bases that rise higher and higher to sway in linguistic breezes that laugh at the seriousness and the solidity, and that puff and puff until the great, ponderous, massive structure of pretentious thought comes crashing, tumbling down to disappear into the crevices and corners of the psyche; uninhibited emotional language that begins to grow in a shapeless, inflated mass, rising and proliferating in lumps and bumps and expanding to a huge suffocating monstrosity, only to be punctured by a sharp linguistic splinter of ridicule, to collapse with a great outrush of air and shrieking sound, and to drip finally away into the darkness beyond consciousness; of language games and language play, of language jokes and language hoaxes, of language hysteria and language outrage, of language sense and language nonsense.

All of this rich inner linguistic life goes on without our willing or wanting, encouraging or directing it. It is ours by right of being human, of being conscious and aware, of living and breathing in a linguistic environment. And it is an important part of what makes us individual human beings, each one different from all others. The interior stream of language is never duplicated from person to person, and never duplicated in the same person from day to day. Like a kaleidoscope of constantly shifting shapes and colors, with no single frame remaining for more than a moment, the linguistic flow offers a complex of ideas, words, phrases, and anti-ideas for a flash of contemplation, and then rushes on to another complex, the old one breaking into parts which rearrange or flow on into the deeper reservoirs of self.

The inner does not become outer, and the outer become inner, just by the rediscovery of the "inner" world. That is only the beginning. As a whole, we are a generation of men so estranged from the inner world that many are arguing that it does not exist; and that even if it does exist, it does not matter. Even if it has some significance, it is not the hard stuff of science, and if it is not, then let's make it hard. Let it be measured and counted. Quantify the heart's agony and ecstasy in a world in which, when the inner world is first discovered, we are liable to find ourselves bereft and derelict. For without the inner the outer loses its meaning, and without the outer the inner loses its substance.

R. D. Laing, *The Politics of Experience*, 1967.

How may we direct our gaze inward, and become spectators of this neverending drama of the interior? Probably this peering within can be done only at the expense of affecting the flow, of adding a dimension and of diverting it into channels that somehow reflect the peering itself, the self-consciousness of the act of witnessing one's own being. Many novelists have been fascinated with the possibilities of dramatizing the linguistic flow by a method that has been variously named the "interior monologue" or "stream-of-consciousness" (a term, incidentally, that William James invented in *The Principles of Psychology*, 1890). A look at some of the ways novelists have dramatized this interior language might help us to penetrate our own exterior crust of formal thought to become observers of and fishers in our own streams.

Probably the most famous use in fiction of stream-of-consciousness appears in James Joyce's *Ulysses,* in the concluding section which presents Molly Bloom's soliloquy. Molly Bloom is the unfaithful wife of the novel's Jewish hero, Leopold, and in her bedtime reverie her mind seems to float free of all its fastenings and to roam at will among fantastic realities and realistic fantasies. Here are the opening lines of some forty pages of mental meanderings: "Yes because he never did a thing like that before as ask to get his breakfast in bed with a couple of eggs since the *City Arms* hotel when he used to be pretending to be laid up with a sick voice doing his highness to make himself interesting to that old faggot Mrs Riordan that he thought he had a great leg of and she never left us a farthing all for masses for herself and her soul greatest miser ever was actually afraid to lay out 4d for her methylated spirit telling me all her ailments she had too much old chat in her about politics and earthquakes and the end of the world let us have a bit of fun first God help the world if all the women were her sort down on bathingsuits and lownecks of course nobody wanted her to wear I suppose she was pious because no man would look at her twice. . . ."[1]

In William Faulkner's *The Sound and the Fury,* young Quentin Compson, at Harvard, wakes up on the day that he will commit suicide—an act obscurely motivated by a complex of causes, including his love for his promiscuous sister, his despair for his disintegrating family, and his inheritance of his father's bleak view of the world. Just awakening to consciousness, trapped in an emotional dilemma that offers no escape, he begins the reverie that will accompany him in his despondency all day: "When the shadow of the sash appeared on the curtains it was between seven

1. James Joyce, *Ulysses* (New York: Random House, 1922; rpt. Modern Library-Random House, 1934), p. 723.

I. LANGUAGE AS CREATION

and eight o'clock and then I was in time again, hearing the watch. It was Grandfather's and when Father gave it to me he said, Quentin, I give you the mausoleum of all hope and desire; it's rather excruciatingly apt that you will use it to gain the reducto absurdum of all human experience which can fit your individual needs no better than it fitted his or his father's. I give it to you not that you may remember time, but that you might forget it now and then for a moment and not spend all your breath trying to conquer it. Because no battle is ever won he said. They are not even fought. The field only reveals to man his own folly and despair, and victory is an illusion of philosophers and fools."[2]

In her most experimental novel, *The Waves,* Virginia Woolf relates the stories of a number of characters—all friends as children—whose lives are loosely intertwined, carrying them from childhood to old age (or death) by moving lightly from one mind to another and simply recording (or rather, dramatizing) the flow of sensations, sights, and insights, letting the plot fend for itself as it might in remembered, recalled, or reviewed events of no large consequence. There is no hero in the usual sense, but prominent among the principal characters is Bernard, the "phrase-maker," who opens the novel as a young boy, and closes it as an elderly man. Here is a passage near the end of the book, from Bernard's point of view: "Again I see before me the usual street. The canopy of civilisation is burnt out. The sky is dark as polished whale-bone. But there is a kindling in the sky whether of lamplight or of dawn. There is a stir of some sort—sparrows on plane trees somewhere chirping. There is a sense of the break of day. I will not call it dawn. What is dawn in the city to an elderly man standing in the street looking up rather dizzily at the sky? Dawn is some sort of whitening of the sky; some sort of renewal. Another day, another Friday; another twentieth of March, January, or September. Another general awakening. The stars draw back and are

2. William Faulkner, *The Sound and the Fury* (New York: Random House, 1929; rpt. Modern Library-Random House, 1946), p. 95.

extinguished. The bars deepen themselves between the waves. The film of mist thickens on the fields. A redness gathers on the roses, even on the pale rose that hangs by the bedroom window. A bird chirps. Cottagers light their early candles. Yes, this is the eternal renewal, the incessant rise and fall and fall and rise again."[3]

These three samples of stream-of-consciousness from three novelists are not presented here as giving the last word as to how language actually flows through the mind. Indeed, on such a matter there can never be a last word. For every mind has its individual flow. And every novelist has his individual view of reality. The point to be made, however, is that there is a flow, that it is made up of a multitude of elements that appear and disappear as much by chance as by design, and that this flow becomes the source of any display of language in which we indulge, whether oral or written. We should not permit this flow to inundate us, nor should we view it as so irrational and sinister as to merit suppression. For a proper attitude, perhaps the novelists can offer us a clue: to view the flow as fascinating and revelatory, offering us a window into our minds and our very selves, and constituting a resource that might be used when we attempt to project ourselves in speech or on paper.

When we set forth in search of an idea, or set of related ideas, what we really begin with is a muddle—that eternal flow of irrational association through the mind. Where in the midst of all those vaguely related impressions and responses, fragmentary feelings, and aborted ideas—where is belief, commitment, conviction? Where indeed? If we are suddenly asked our opinion about God, or our view of socialism, or our thinking about the police, we can pluck at once something floating by in the stream and provide an answer, or we can await the surging to the surface of some old attitudes conditioned by forgotten or only dimly remem-

3. Virginia Woolf, *The Waves* (New York: Harcourt Brace Jovanovich, 1931; rpt. Harvest-Harcourt), pp. 382–83.

bered experiences and offer the questioner sets of words and phrases whose meaning remains unexamined and possibly incoherent. Or we can let the question become a seine, arrange it in the stream for its catch, and then examine and sort through what the net has caught, using the experience as a way of finding out what we *really* think, what we *really* believe, what and who we really are, and what we might come to think and believe. Such examining or sorting through can no doubt be painful, as when we discover in the net an unrealized prejudice or irrational hatred; or it can be pleasant, as when we find unexpected generosities and impulsive kindliness. But painful or pleasant, the experience must prove valuable as a process of rediscovery and reshaping of the ever changing, always becoming, enigmatic self.

Ideas and Experiments

1. Observe as closely as possible your own language flow for a day, and write an account of its changing patterns and emphases. What are the impressions or suggestions most instrumental in determining direction of the flow?

2. Confronted with a blank sheet of paper, begin to write everything that comes into your mind. Since you will be thinking about your thinking, you'll have to stand off some distance so as not to intrude too much. Otherwise, all your thoughts will be absorbed merely with the attempts to observe your thoughts. Pretend that you are a novelist writing about your mind flow. After recording some paragraphs of it, give an objective description of the circumstances related to the flow of language.

3. Assume the role of a novelist and dramatize the stream-of-consciousness of someone you know or imagine—even yourself if you can envision yourself as an imaginary person. A teacher standing before a class . . . a student writing an examination . . . a doctor performing surgery . . . an old woman in a rocking chair before a window . . . a young wife cooking the evening meal. . . .

4. Emerson said: "A foolish consistency is the hobgoblin of little minds, adored by little statesmen and philosophers and divines." Watch the flow of your mind until you catch it in an inconsistency—of feeling, attitude, idea. Examine the causes insofar as you can determine them. You want to go and you do not want to go some place . . . you agree and you disagree . . . you are pleased but you are also ashamed. . . .

5. Rethink one of your deepest beliefs. Bring it to the surface of your mind and let the stream flow around and through it. Delve as deeply as you can to the roots of this belief. See what discovery you can make as to why you believe what you believe, what complex set of associations accompany the belief, what would have to happen before you could change the belief. If this is too painful, think back to a time when you did change your mind, shift your belief. Can you reconstruct the stream of that time?

Further Points of Departure

1. Read one of the novels quoted here, or another novel that uses the stream-of-consciousness technique, and write a sketch of a character on the basis of the revelations of his mind.

2. Write a narrative in which you record a conversation between two people. After each speech, in parentheses, indicate the contents of the mind of the speaker that are omitted from the speech.

3. Write a poem in the form of a meditation on or musing about some subject which moves you deeply—love, death, pain, injustice. Catch if you can some of the inconsistencies, vagaries, or whimsicalities of the mind as it plays about a subject. You might find you'll do best by starting with a specific event that has affected you directly—an actual death, a concrete injustice, some terrible suffering.

3. Person, Place, and Thing

. . . while [language] may be looked upon as a symbolic system which reports or refers to or otherwise substitutes for direct experience, it does not as a matter of actual behavior stand apart from or run parallel to direct experience but completely interpenetrates with it.

It is this constant interplay between language and experience which removes language from the cold status of such purely and simply symbolic systems as mathematical symbolism or flag signaling. This interpenetration is not only an intimate associative fact; it is also a contextual one. It is important to realize that language may not only refer to experience or even mold, interpret, and discover experience, but that it also substitutes for it in the sense that in those sequences of interpersonal behavior which form the greater part of our daily lives speech and action supplement each other and do each other's work in a web of unbroken pattern.

Edward Sapir, "Language," 1933.

And you want to travel with him,
And you want to travel blind,
And you think you'll maybe trust him
'Cause he touched your perfect body
With his mind.

Leonard Cohen, "Suzanne," 1966.

As language flows ceaselessly within the self, helping to define and delimit the interior world of the self in the process, so it also flows ceaselessly (or almost so) from the inside to the world around and beyond the self, also helping to define and delimit and delineate *that* world—a world made up (as in the old definition of a noun) of persons, places, things. Language plays a primary role in connecting us with the persons, places, and things of the universe, and not only in connecting, but also in arranging and ordering. Let us imagine a scene—a particular *place* made particular by specific *things*, where *persons* are enmeshed in complex interactions. As we enter this setting, we discover quickly that it is language that enables us to discriminate and contain the scene, to explore the interrelations of people and their surroundings, and (most important) to discover our own relationship with other human beings as well as the world that contains them. In sum, it is language that in some sense *creates* the scene—in the sense, that is, of giving it a coherence, a center with boundaries, and of investing it with interest and meaning.

Probably the most vital role of language is in its serving as the basis for the interrelationship of all human beings. We admire and we ridicule, we hate and we love—in language. Moreover, language serves as the substance of the web that holds together in intricate patterns social groups, small and large, national and international. But in this as in every sphere, language is much more than merely communicative—it is creative. We create ourselves, our relationships, our friends and enemies, our neighbors and acquaintances, through language.

If it is true, as the Jewish philosopher Martin Buber asserts, that the individual defines himself only in relation to others, that the "I" becomes possible and self-consciously aware only as that "I" is reflected in the eyes of others and the world, then language bears the burden not only of establishing fundamental relationships, but also of tracing the configuration of that "I" and the world. In *I and Thou* Buber wrote: "Through the *Thou* a man becomes *I*. That which confronts him comes and disappears, relational events condense, then are scattered, and in the change consciousness of the unchanging partner, of the *I*, grows clear, and each time stronger. To be sure, it is still seen caught in the web of the relation with the *Thou*, as the increasingly distinguishable feature of that which reaches out to and yet is not the *Thou*. But it continually breaks through with more power, till a time comes when it bursts its bonds, and the *I* confronts itself for a moment, separated as though it were a *Thou;* as quickly to take possession of itself and from then on to enter into relations in conciousness of itself."[4] Martin Buber was concerned about the establishment of "I-Thou" relationships in addition to "I-It" relationships. Although the concept is too metaphysical and elusive to pursue here (see Buber's classic book, *I and Thou*), it is enough for our purposes to take note of his insight that the self defines itself only relationally—as the self interacts in all the encounters of experience: "I discover who I am through exploration of all the relationships of my experience, for I am created only in the experiences of those relationships."

In all human relationships, language is thus crucial and creative. Correctness (or, in the popular concept, "good grammar") has nothing to do with language fulfilling its creative role in these relationships. The creativity is sustained not by language that is correct or "proper" but rather by language that is in some sense genuine. Walt Whitman's poem, "A Noiseless Patient Spider," may be read symbolically as a poem about human relationships initiated and sustained through the launched "filaments" of language, whether comprised of words or gestures or both:

A noiseless patient spider,
I mark'd where on a little promontory it stood isolated,
Mark'd how to explore the vacant vast surrounding,

4. Martin Buber, *I and Thou* (New York: Charles Scribner's Sons, 1958), pp. 28–29.

It launch'd forth filament, filament, filament, out of itself,
Ever unreeling them, ever tirelessly speeding them.

And you O my soul where you stand,
Surrounded, detached, in measureless oceans of space,
Ceaselessly musing, venturing, throwing, seeking the spheres
    to connect them,
Till the bridge you will need be form'd, till the ductile anchor
    hold,
Till the gossamer thread you fling catch somewhere, O my
    soul.[5]

"Ceaselessly musing, venturing, throwing"—thus we all live out
our lives, spin out the web of our existence, create the patterns
of relationships that tell us who we are and what the world for us
appears to be.

With language we not only discover and create ourselves, we
discover and create the people who make up our lives. It has often
been observed that a man is doomed to live out his life in isolation, in the loneliness of his impenetrable life, because no man can
ever bare his soul completely to another, no man can ever really
know another. It has also often been observed that each man lives
many lives, plays many roles, assumes many characters—with one
role frequently preserved for one special relationship. A man is
one person to his children, another to his wife, another to his business associates, and still another to his employer. These are only
a few of his roles—and he had still others in his boyhood, and will
have still others as he accumulates years. Who, finally, is the real
person, the actual individual? The question may appear unan-
swerable, but we constantly answer it for ourselves in the progress of daily living: we create versions for ourselves of the people
we know out of both casual encounters and fragmentary experiences with them. We carry linguistic images of these people

5. Walt Whitman, *Complete Poetry and Selected Prose,* ed. James E.
Miller, Jr. (Boston: Houghton Mifflin Co., 1959), p. 314.

I. LANGUAGE AS CREATION

around in our memories and imaginations which we accept as reality, and we are often surprised when we compare our image of Smith or Jones with the image projected by a mutual friend. We may reject the new image, or adjust our own impression to embrace the new fragment. But whatever we do, the point is that through language, we create the people in our lives.

> **I gotta use words when I talk to you**
> **But if you understand or if you dont**
> **That's nothing to me and nothing to you**
> **We all gotta do what we gotta do**
> T. S. Eliot, "Sweeney Agonistes"
> [Sweeney speaking to Doris], 1927.

Underpinning and supporting these creative relationships with persons are creative relationships with places and things—with, in short, all the contents of the world and the universe. We do not, of course, *physically* create the places we inhabit or the objects we encounter—unless we are craftsmen of special sorts (and even then we are "creators" in a very limited sense). But we do create —or recreate them—in the linguistic imagination, and it is in that incarnation that they become the actuality with which we cope and the reality that clings in the memory.

There is an old party game in which all the participants are led into an unfamiliar room, left for a short time (perhaps a minute or two), and then brought out and asked to write down a description and a list of contents of the room: It is always amazing to discover the radical differences in the rooms recreated by the participating players. And the differences are not caused by some being "right" and others being "wrong." In a sense, all the versions are right and all are wrong. All the versions are right in that they represent impressions that by their very nature are selective; all are wrong in that the room and its contents are so complex and multitudinous in reality that no set of impressions, even if they were endless, could exhaust the possibilities of their combinations, interrelations, emanations, or emotional vibrations. Moreover, even the untouched room changes throughout the day with the shifting sun, and offers different shapes, shades, and proportions to individuals in different parts of the space. And the different backgrounds, interests, moods, and emotional dispositions of the observers will determine what is observed, how it is observed, and how it is remembered.

This old-fashioned fun-game has its counterpart in serious experience every day in courts of law, particularly in testimony accumulated in cases of automobile accidents—in cases tried to determine fault. It is legendary that there are as many versions of an accident as there are witnesses. And it is futile to search for one true version among many false ones. It is more likely possible that the truth—that is, the "truth" for purposes of establishing fault—will emerge by some creative collation of several versions. Such a collation would be possible, however, only if all the versions were honest (as distinguished from "true"). But even if some version of the truth should be arrived at by the court, the truth "in reality" of a particular accident will not even be approached. We might come nearer to it if we retained novelists to probe the interior lives of those involved, and if we found poets to explore the impact of the accident on disrupted plans or crippled lives. These are matters with which courts have little to do. But even with these versions added, there would remain aspects and dimensions that would go untouched.

The persons, places, and things of our lives of course have a solid physical existence of their own, which anybody in encounter with them would deny at peril of stubbing his toe or bruising his

> The world's contents are <u>given</u> to each of us in an order so foreign to our subjective interests that we can hardly by an effort of the imagination picture to ourselves what it is like. We have to break that order altogether,—and by picking out from it the items which concern us, and connecting them with others far away, which we say "belong" with them, we are able to make out definite threads of sequence and tendency; to foresee particular liabilities and get ready for them; and to enjoy simplicity and harmony in place of what was chaos. Is not the sum of your actual experience taken at this moment and impartially added together an utter chaos?
>
> William James, "Reflex Action and Theism,"
> *The Will to Believe*, 1897.

ego. But, again, the realities we live with are these that we create in the linguistic imagination and carry about with us in mind and memory. We turn a person into a friend, a place into a room for reverie, a thing into a keepsake charged with strong feelings. And we write all of these into the running narrative of our ceaselessly flowing, continuously altering lives.

Ideas and Experiments

1. Explore the human relationships of your life. How many roles do you think you play? How many versions of yourself are you able to define? Write an essay in which you describe your various identities in your various roles.

2. Observe a person close to you, and discover how many roles he plays. What is the role he plays with you? How does he change

in the presence of others? Write an account of his various versions of himself.

3. Keep a close account of yourself on a single day. How many times did you change roles? Make a record of your various feelings—your moments of awareness, of frustration, of befuddlement, of dejection, of exuberance. Write a profile of yourself for the day, exploring the question as to the nature of the real you.

4. Observe closely the way you use language in one or more of your relationships. Keep an account of what was actually said in moments of emotional intensity, pleasant or unpleasant. Then analyze the exchange of language: did the language stay on the surface of the moment or incident? Or did it interpenetrate the experience and become the experience? Probe as deeply as you can the relationship of the language to the experience, considering particularly its shaping of the experience and its substitution for it.

5. Collect various impressions of an individual from mutual acquaintances. What may account for the variety? Write a multiple-character sketch of the person—that is, describe him several times, each time as he is seen by a different person, someone who knows him, emphasizing the ways in which he seems to be a different person to different people. Conclude with an account of how your impressions have been modified by your awareness of the impressions of others.

Further Points of Departure

1. Write a two-part story in which two different people see and experience a scene or event in two radically different ways because of radically different emotional states. Perhaps you will want to make one of the characters male, the other female; perhaps one is old, the other young; perhaps one is bright, one dumb.

2. Find a newspaper account of a single event—a robbery, rape, or accident. Construct a story which will use the newspaper

account as an accurate public account of the conclusion, but tell the story first from the point of view of one of the people involved, perhaps using the first person as a form of narration. Suggest in your story the complexity of feeling and attitude and emotional involvement that is left out of the newspaper account. Show how the lives of your characters were deeply affected or changed in ways not mentioned in the news story. For an example to use as a model, see James Joyce's short story, "A Painful Case," in his volume of stories *Dubliners*. Or for a more complicated and longer example, see Herman Melville's *Billy Budd*.

4. Creating Order Out of Chaos

The real world as it is given objectively at this moment is the sum total of all its beings and events now. But can we think of such a sum? Can we realize for an instant what a cross-section of all existence at a definite point of time would be? While I talk and the flies buzz, a sea gull catches a fish at the mouth of the Amazon, a tree falls in the Adirondack wilderness, a man sneezes in Germany, a horse dies in Tartary, and twins are born in France. What does it mean? Does the contemporaneity of these events with one another, and with a million others as disjointed, form a rational bond between them, and unite them into anything that means for us a world? Yet just such a collateral contemporaneity, and nothing else, is the real order of the world. It is an order with which we have nothing to do but to get away from it as fast as possible. As I said, we break it: we break it into histories, and we break it into arts, and we break it into sciences; and then we begin to feel at home. We make ten thousand separate serial orders of it, and on any one of these we react as though the others did not exist.

William James, "Reflex Action and Theism,"
The Will to Believe, 1897.

Life itself, or experience, is infinitely more complex than simple persons, places, or things. We use language as a defense against this complexity. If we were forced to cope with the total incoherence, disconnectedness, and irrationality of human experience and life each day afresh, we should all go mad. We avoid this random flux and flow by living within structures and by structures that are created and sustained primarily by language. We create order linguistically out of the chaos of experience.

Simply by its selective nature, language reduces the vast and awesome overabundance of life as daily encountered to manageable proportions. However much scholars have disagreed about the nature of language, they have agreed that it is symbolic. The written language is symbolic of sounds, and the sounds of language are symbolic of aspects of life and experience, whether real or imagined. Symbols by their very nature are abstractive and reductive, throwing things and elements together in classes and groups; glossing over subtle or minute distinctions to get at essences; transforming complexities into simplicities by selecting main feature, principle aspects, dominant traits. We walk into the woods by a pond on a sunny, summer day, and the details of the landscape that clamor for the attention of the senses of sight, smell, touch are so multitudinous as to be beyond count—their subtle shadings and infinite combinations requiring a lifetime or more to measure and record—but we say simply, "What a beautiful day! Look at that blue sky, that water . . . the trees." We attempt, in short, to suggest symbolically in language something of the nature of the total experience of the woods on a particular occasion by a severe selection of a few dominant features—but, of course, we use tone of voice, gesture, posture, perhaps even a touch or caress, all to help express our feeling. As experience becomes more complicated than a simple stroll through the woods, the challenge to grasp and convey something of its nature in language becomes even greater.

And in fact, in real life, when you meet somebody in the street you don't start recording that she had this sort of nose—at least a man doesn't. I mean, if you're the sort of person that meets a girl in the street and instantly notices the color of her eyes and of her hair and the sort of dress she's wearing, then you're not in the least like me. I just notice a feeling from people. I notice particularly the cadence of their voices, the sort of phrases they'll use, and that's what I'm all the time trying to hear in my head, how people word things—because everybody speaks an entirely different language, that's really what it amounts to.

Frank O'Connor, *Writers at Work: The Paris Review Interviews,* 1958.

Similarly we attempt to simplify the enigmas and complexities of life by adopting conventions of language-use that have the nature of rituals. A simple example is the universal human greetings of "how do you do" and "how are you," phrases that are not to be taken seriously as to meaning but are taken nevertheless very seriously as social gestures and signals. Even the reply, "I'm fine, how are you," must be recognized not as a statement of well being and solicitude but as part of the ritual of human encounter that reestablishes temporarily interrupted relationships. Such ritualistic exchanges run through all our social relationships, and are not (as sometimes supposed) examples of gross hypocrisy but rather are linguistic structures universally recognized as appropriate for certain situations—as meaningful (or meaningless) as shaking hands on coming together or waving hands at departure. These structures are but the simplest examples of such linguistic structures. At their most stylized and formal such structures can become oaths of fealty or allegiance that are recited in unison, or set prayers read aloud by a congregation from a prayer book during a church service. In between the casual greeting and the formalized group recitation are innumerable linguistic structures that give shape and form to our life, cushioning the shock of each day's strange, new, and potentially bewildering experience. Shared jokes that are ritualistically retold, bawdy and scatalogical language signaling a shared male understanding, a TV news program that presents a "round-up" of the day's devastating news in a set format or pattern—all of these and multitudes of other linguistic structures provide havens from the rage of natural disorder that could, if not placed under linguistic control, if not reduced to human dimensions graspable by the human imagination, tear our lives to pieces.

What other response than anguish, followed by anesthesia and then by wit and the elevating of intelligence over sentiment, is possible as a response to the social disorder and mass atrocities of our time, and—equally important for our sensibilities, but less often remarked on—to the unprecedented change in what rules our environment from the intelligible and visible to that which is only with difficulty intelligible, and is invisible?

Susan Sontag, "One Culture and the New Sensibility," *Against Interpretation*, 1966.

But though language lends itself to the conventions of linguistic structures, and serves us by providing a daily refuge of the familiar in the midst of the continually new, it lends itself also to the nonconventional and nonrepetitive, and serves us perhaps

I. LANGUAGE AS CREATION

even more by providing us paths of awareness into the unfamiliar, the strange, the alien. Language may be viewed as a sixth sense, embracing all the others and providing a dimension of experience beyond the reach of all of them. We apprehend the world by use of our senses—sight, sound, smell, taste, feel—but we apprehend it most fully and with most profound awareness through language, as it imposes an order on the inundated senses, and creates a structure which may be accepted as the meaning of an incident or event. However we "interpret" an experience, it must be finally in language.

Average human consciousness sometimes needs to be shocked out of its dullness or density, its habitual imperceptiveness. Much poetry is devoted to ferreting out the strange that lies within the realm of the familiar. It is true that we are often so caught up in the dailiness of the daily, so dulled by routines and bound by conventions that we cannot see to see, cannot structure for ourselves the unique moment or passing scene, and simply accept an available structure, a secondhand sight. William Carlos Williams made much of his poetry out of scenes and objects that many of us would have passed over or by without so much as a glance. For example—

The Red Wheelbarrow

> so much depends
> upon
>
> a red wheel
> barrow
>
> glazed with rain
> water
>
> beside the white
> chickens[6]

6. William Carlos Williams, *The Collected Earlier Poems* (New York: New Directions, 1951), p. 277.

Clearly this simple set of images is highly selective. A complete —or more nearly complete—catalogue of objects that must have been in the scene would alter the experience implied by the severity of this selection, with its emphasis on color and texture and concrete elements—barrow, water, chickens. Whatever Williams actually saw on some particular occasion, he created the scene through language by selecting and arranging in a particular order the details upon which, as he says, "so much depends." Just what depends, we are not told; that remains subjective, Williams's secret, the motive-force that spurs him to the linguistic creation or recreation of the scene and moment.

. . . human language, in its normal use, is free from the control of independently identifiable external stimuli or internal states and is not restricted to any practical communicative function, in contrast, for example, to the pseudo language of animals. It is thus free to serve as an instrument of free thought and self-expression. The limitless possibilities of thought and imagination are reflected in the creative aspect of language use.
Noam Chomsky, *Cartesian Linguistics,* 1966.

What Williams does in "The Red Wheelbarrow"—in abstracting, simplifying, and ordering a scene—we all do constantly in our everyday encounter with life, in our recurring entanglements in the tangled webs of experience. We walk down the street of a modern city on a smoggy day. As we walk we are the moving center of an unfolding narrative which we ourselves write in un-

I. LANGUAGE AS CREATION

spoken language. Our awareness is not wide enough, however, to catch every element of the experience. We push the throngs to the periphery of attention and observe a child holding back on an adult, a dog that almost interrupts our stride, a blind beggar with a tin cup, a pregnant young woman perspiring at the temples, two dark-suited gentlemen in earnest conversation. Accompanying these fleeting and random sights are views of store windows crammed successively with office equipment (a typewriter receives a glance), books (a single title presses on consciousness), ties (a tie sale), men's and women's suits (a print of dominant pink flashes past), and many more. The traffic moves ceaselessly in the streets, in a parade of automobiles that break through consciousness with their sounds and noises, their colors and shapes and kinds; a long, sleek limousine, with a lady in a broad-brimmed blue hat in the back seat, hangs for a moment on the edge of vision; a white ambulance makes its way carefully through the traffic; a red bakery truck jerks to a stop by the curb. Along the edge of the street lies the discarded refuse of the hurrying crowds —candy wrappers, cigarette packages, fragments of newspapers, a broken bottle. . . .

If an attempt to catalogue the totality of but a simple walk down the street is doomed to failure, a more complex experience would be still more dependent on—and thankful for—language's rage for order. Language both forces and enables selection, ordering, focusing. Through its use, a multitude of impressions that rush in and ambush the senses can be sifted and sorted.

Such is the nature of language in its complex interpenetration of experience that it may be said to *create* the experience in the sense of giving it form and shape—making of experience an embodiment that may be held in the mind for understanding and recollection. In its most fundamental role language is thus creative—a role that must be stressed as underlying and supporting its more commonly recognized roles as expressive and communicative.

Ideas and Experiments

1. Find a scene, like the one in the Williams poem, and note first the sheer density of it—objects, elements, relationships, colors, textures, shapes, movements. Describe it as fully as language will allow. Then attempt to "embody" it with the severity of selection of the Williams poem. Try several versions, compare them, and explore their comparative merits.

2. Observe your own language-use for one or two days and note the occasions on which you rely on language-conventions for social intercourse. Report the conversations as they were actually experienced, and then imagine them had the participants refused to use the conventions and insisted on ruthless honesty and literal use of language.

3. Explore the ways in which language creates experience by trying, after some significant human encounter (involving hate, love, argument, quarreling, being caught in a lie, caught stealing, caught giving money to a beggar) to recreate the event as understood and stored in the memory of the various participants. Then play God and attempt to present an "objective" (absolutely impersonal) version of what happened.

Further Points of Departure

1. Write a short story into which you weave a red wheelbarrow, rain, and white chickens. Perhaps there has been a mysterious burial on a farm, or a farmhand has disappeared on a rainy night, or the sound of chickens has aroused a farmer's wife just in time, or a young son has died. . . . Begin or end your story with the Williams poem.

2. Try your hand at writing a deliberately bad and perhaps even sentimental poem, of substantial length, in which you take the ingredients in the Williams poem (red wheelbarrow, rain, white chickens) and weave them into a beautiful scene, in con-

fronting which you cannot contain your emotions; or into an ugly scene, which repels you deeply; or into a sad scene, which makes you want to cry. In each case attempt to take your cue from the opening line, "so much depends. . . ." Your poem might explain in fulsome detail what it is that "depends."

3. Or, if you feel incapable of writing a bad poem (called for in 2 above), write a deliberately good poem along the same lines, but with genuine rather than spurious emotions.

II. WRITING, THINKING, AND FEELING

1. Language and Thought

The relation of thought to word is not a thing but a process, a continual movement back and forth from thought to word and from word to thought. In that process the relation of thought to word undergoes changes which themselves may be regarded as development in the functional sense. Thought is not merely expressed in words; it comes into existence through them. Every thought tends to connect something with something else, to establish a relationship between things.

The structure of speech does not simply mirror the structure of thought; that is why words cannot be put on by thought like a ready-made garment. Thought undergoes many changes as it turns into speech. It does not merely find expression in speech; it finds its reality and form.

A speaker often takes several minutes to disclose one thought. In his mind the whole thought is present at once, but in speech it has to be developed successively. A thought may be compared to a cloud shedding a shower of words.

The relation between thought and word is a living process; thought is born through words. A word devoid of thought is a dead thing, and a thought unembodied in words remains a shadow. The connection between them, however, is not a preformed and constant one. It emerges in the course of development, and itself evolves.

L. S. Vygotsky, *Thought and Language*, 1962.

"How do I know what I mean until I see what I say?" This exclamation has been good for a chuckle for a long time. But it has also been good for suggesting a problem that has puzzled men for a long time: what is the relationship between saying and thinking, between language and thought? Looked at one way, language appears to be simply the clothing of naked thought. But looked at another way, language and thought appear inseparable —a particular thought expressed in particular words cannot be expressed in any other words without subtly changing meaning and impact. Just thinking about the difficulties of translation from one language to another makes the problem clear. It is true that there is successful translation, and that the thought of a piece in English can be expressed in German, Russian, or Chinese. But at the same time translators are the first to point out that there are immense difficulties in translation; and though the gross substance of thought can be transferred from one language to another, the nuances, subtleties, and delicate complexities are frequently lost in the process.

Translation from one language to another is but a more extreme version of translation within a language, from one set of words to another. It is a commonplace that poetry cannot be translated without radical change of the poem. Robert Frost defined poetry as that which was lost in the translation. Of all literary forms, poetry is the most dependent on those nuances and shadings so easily destroyed by a bit of bungling with the words. It is also a commonplace that to paraphrase a poem constitutes a "heresy." Paraphrasing is merely the process of exchanging one set of words for another set of words, supposedly without changing the "meaning" or "thought." But everyone knows the impossibility of this task—meaning and thought may in some gross sense remain the same, but where they may live in their original delicacy of gradation, they simply die in the operation of paraphrase, just as they do in translation.

If, then, thought and language are so firmly welded together, how can they be different?

> **Let it be admitted then that language is not the essence of thought. But this conclusion must be carefully limited. Apart from language, the retention of thought, the easy recall of thought, the interweaving of thought into higher complexity, the communication of thought, are all gravely limited.**
> Alfred North Whitehead,
> *Modes of Thought*, 1938.

For they are different—in some sense. Experiments with the development of children's language have shown that thoughts precede speech. A child desires to have a toy dangling before his eyes. The desire may be translated into the simple sentence, "I want that." But the child cannot speak. He reaches out for the toy, and when it is removed to a position outside his reach, the frustrated child begins to cry. In brief, the child has had a thought —"I want that." But he has not expressed the thought in language, to himself or to others. He *has* expressed his thought by body-movement and gesture. He has communicated his desire without language.

Therefore, thought and language are not absolutely identical. But neither are they absolutely different. The child's thought, in the example above, is of the grossest sort, indistinguishable from desire. When we place that thought, expressible without language, beside the thought of, say, the philosopher, or historian, or psychologist, or sociologist, we seem to have a difference not only of magnitude but also of kind. Abstractions and generalizations —meditations about the fickleness of women or the elusiveness of truth—seem well nigh inconceivable without language. And thought without some abstraction and generalization is likely to appear somewhat elementary, if not gross.

> I used to spend a lot of time worrying over word order, trying to create beautiful passages. I still believe in the value of a handsome style. I appreciate the sensibility which can produce a nice turn of phrase, like Scott Fitzgerald. But I'm not interested any more in turning out something shimmering and impressionistic—Southern, if you will—full of word-pictures, damn Dixie baby-talk, and that sort of thing. I guess I just get more and more interested in people. And story.
>
> William Styron, *Writers at Work: The Paris Review Interviews*, 1958.

Thought and language, then, may best be viewed as an interlocking process, not quite identical, but not entirely separable. And as subtlety and complexity increase, the relationship of language and thought becomes so close and intimate as to defeat division. The widely held view, that thought is basically the body while language is merely its dress, and therefore variable, is highly misleading. Language is much more fundamental: if thought is the body, language is better viewed as the food and drink that gives it sustenance and enables it to grow, to mature, to go forth in the world under its own power, and with its own strength. And as the nourishment turns into blood and tissue, bone and muscle, so language is assimilated into thought and the two together have a united vitality.

All this is not to say that language is always thought. When language is used primarily as convention ("How do you do?" "I'm fine, how are you?"), it is largely void of thought, and is primarily ritualistic behavior. Language can be used for many purposes other than communicating thought—for expressing emotion, for exploring embryonic ideas, for talking nonsense to one's self. And language can be used to disguise and hide thought. In social situations, we frequently find ourselves using language to conceal as much as to reveal. This kind of behavior is universal and is not confined to hypocrites. If everyone at all times spoke his mind continuously and fully, without regard for the feelings of others, it is doubtful that social intercourse could continue. We all learn very early in life to use language not just for conveying ideas, thoughts, and emotions, but—especially in social situations —for developing or deepening relationships with other people. We tell stories to evoke interest, we make up jokes to evoke laughter, we spout nonsense to fill silences, and we even, on occasion, "whisper sweet nothings."

The language of ordinary social intercourse is so ambiguous in meaning and so oblique in intent that one great dramatic director, Stanislavsky, required his actors to discover what he called the "subtext" of the dialogue of a play, the meaning of the lines that exists not in the literal sense of the words but in the subtle implications. An obvious example may be cited from *Macbeth*, when Macbeth tells Lady Macbeth: "My dearest love, Duncan comes here tonight." She replies: "And when goes hence?" The actor playing Macbeth will realize that the subtext beneath the simple statement suggests that there will be an opportunity, in King Duncan's visit, for the murder that both have vaguely in mind but have not discussed. Lady Macbeth's

II. WRITING, THINKING, AND FEELING

reply—"And when goes hence?"—may be innocent-seeming on the surface, but the subtext may be something of a taunt to her husband to summon the courage to kill the king—so that he may never go "hence," or so that he may "go" in the sense of "depart this life." When actors come to understand the subtext of the play, they can then give the interpretation that makes for great performances.

> An artist, any artist, must say where it is in the world that he actually is. And by doing this he will also say who he is. But no matter what a man tries, the products of his thinking, indeed of his life, will identify who and where. . . .
>
> LeRoi Jones,
> "LeRoi Jones Talking,"
> Home: Social Essays, 1966.

Conversations in real life also have their subtexts, their flow of meaning beneath the actual words that are spoken. All of us are attuned to these subtexts, to recognizing meanings that are unspoken, and to replying in language that implies, or suggests, or hints at meanings other than the literal. When someone says, "Oh, what an *interesting* jacket you are wearing," the inflection may indicate that the real meaning is: "Your jacket is loud and flashy, and is another indication of your poor taste in clothes." The reply might run: "Do you *really* like it? I bought it to go with the maroon slacks I have." This might indicate: "I know you think it too flashy, and I realize its colors are intense, but I *did* have color-harmony in mind when I bought it." All of us have experienced situations in which what was said meant precisely its opposite—when, "Please, don't tell me any more about it" meant "go on with the story," and when "Stop your teasing" meant "Keep up the joking, I am enjoying it."

The relationship of thought to language is, thus, a complicated one. The exclamation "How do I know what I mean until I see what I say?" may be taken seriously as recognition of this complicated relationship. But we might add to the exclamation: "Even when I see what I say, I may have to dig beneath the words to find what I mean." Thought and language flow together in an interconnected process that would quickly collapse in the absence of either. Thought is a spur to language, and language in turn becomes a spur to thought, and as the two combine in the gradual development of an elaborate structure, their interdependence becomes all the more clear. Thought without language remains blunt and gross; language without thought remains inert and dead. Brought together in the right relationship, thought breathes life into language, while language grants grace, shape, form, and subtlety to thought.

Ideas and Experiments

1. Look up two or more different translations of the same work, and explore the effect of the differences. Is the basic thought altered in the various versions? Are subtleties of thought altered? If you know the original language, check the translations against the original work, and discuss the difficulties faced by the translators.

2. Find or write a series of paraphrases of a poem or a paragraph of prose. Discuss the alterations of thought that come with the alterations of language.

3. Examine your own language for a day, with special attention to the subtexts of your speeches. How frequently do you depend on unspoken meanings, and why? Speculate as to what would

have happened had you spoken with absolute honesty, with literal meaning foremost, for the whole day.

4. Recreate a conversation that you have overheard or in which you have participated, and then supply a plausible subtext. You will need to use your imagination to penetrate to the delicately balanced relationships of all the people involved.

5. Discuss the relationship between thought and language in the following sayings taken from Benjamin Franklin's *Poor Richard's Almanac:*

    a. If you would know the value of money, go and try to borrow some.

    b. 'Tis hard for an empty bag to stand upright.

    c. Let thy maid-servant be faithful, strong, and homely.

    d. Fish and visitors smell in three days.

    e. If you would have a faithful servant, and one that you like, serve yourself.

Further Points of Departure

1. The following quotation is taken from Hermann Hesse's *Demian,* Chapter 5: "The bird fights its way out of the egg. The egg is the world. Who would be born must first destroy a world. The bird flies to God. That God's name is Abraxas."[1] Write a brief narrative which you present as a dramatization of this symbolic and cryptic statement. Or read Hesse's novel and explain the meaning of the quotation in the context of the novel.

2. J. D. Salinger uses the following Zen koan (question a Zen master poses to his student) as an epigraph for his *Nine Stories:* "We know the sound of two hands clapping. But what is the sound of one hand clapping?"[2] (a) write a story or a poem about

1. Hermann Hesse, *Demian: The Story of Emil Sinclair's Youth* (New York: Harper & Row, 1965; rpt. New York: Bantam Books, 1966), p. 76.
2. J. D. Salinger, *Nine Stories* (Boston: Little, Brown, 1953; rpt. New York: Bantam Books, 1964), p. vii.

an individual who suddenly discovers that he is able to hear the sound of one hand clapping; (b) read Salinger's *Nine Stories* and explore in an essay the meaning of the epigraph in its relation to the stories.

2. *Thought and Feeling*

At best, human thought is but a tiny, grammar-bound island, in the midst of a sea of feeling expressed by "Oh-oh" and sheer babble. The island has a periphery, perhaps, of mud—factual and hypothetical concepts broken down by the motional tides into the "material modex," a mixture of meaning and nonsense. Most of us live the better part of our lives on this mud-flat; but in artistic moods we take to the deep, where we flounder about with symptomatic cries that sound like propositions about life and death, good and evil, substance, beauty, and other non-existent topics.

Susanne K. Langer, *Philosophy in a New Key,* 1951.

The mind works in mysterious ways, and thoughts are not so easily summoned or marshalled in ranks as some rhetoricians have said. If thoughts were little soldiers, well-disciplined and obedient, we would have the orderly, intellectual world which has been more frequently described than actually experienced. But thoughts for most of mankind are not soldiers but rowdy children, capricious and undisciplined. They romp into view and quickly vanish around dark corners. They peer from behind decaying tree stumps, make grotesque faces, and fade from sight. Some of the timid ones remain in the distance, almost out of sight, and scurry into underbrush when approached. Some have idiot faces and emit shrill moronic laughter. Some are sober, somber, and slightly pompous, puffed up with self-importance. Still others are pale and ghostly, sleepless, sad-eyed, dragging themselves slowly across the horizon.

These and many more crowd our poor brains, and to put them in order requires boundless patience and energy. Outlines are of little avail. It is good, of course, to see a subject divide into a sequence of parts, but the most detailed outline is of little use if the language flow cannot be started. To seize some of these random thoughts and plant them on paper—this may be the key to inspiration. For there is a strange phenomenon about the flow of thoughts and language that every writer must soon learn: the more thoughts are summoned, seized, and put to use, the more others swarm into the brain as replacements. Every writer who has gotten over his initial panic has at some time experienced this feeling of interior proliferation, this feeling of an abundance so great that it must of its own will burst forth. Putting some of the crowding thoughts down on paper may have the same effect as priming the pump: to begin with a trickle that will lead to full flow.

However much is put down on paper initially to prime the pump or to bring some semblance of order out of the jumble of tumbling thoughts, whenever the act of writing actually begins it is likely not to be a smooth and continual movement through an orderly arrangement of parts, but rather a series of spurts, side-movements, weird reversals—a jerky movement of stop and go that makes for a rather rocky ride. It is in this process that surprises lurk and discoveries are made. We discover thoughts we never suspected we had or could have, and we are surprised by attitudes that we didn't know existed within us. Most experienced writers agree that it is best to drive through to the end, even when the end seems some kind of contradiction of the beginning—and this happens more frequently than has been revealed. A first draft will have its rough spots, lapses, paradoxes, outright conflicts—but it will also represent a thinking and muddling through that is invaluable. Run through the mind again with the thought-processes turned on and testing throughout, it can become the basis of a good piece of writing.

When they finally begin to swarm, where do the thoughts come from on which writing is entirely dependent? Is there a logic-machine that manufactures them when the right buttons are pushed? Or is there a great emotional sponge that, when squeezed, oozes views and attitudes that come sighing and seething to the surface?

It is astonishing how little is known about the working of the mind. But however little or much is known, it is fairly clear that the model of the logic-machine is not only wrong but mischievous. There are people who profess to believe that man can live by logic alone. If only, they say, men developed their reason, looked at all situations and dilemmas logically, and proceeded to devise rational solutions, all human problems would be solved. Be reasonable. Think logically. Act rationally. This line of thought is very persuasive, not to say seductive. It is astonishing, however, how frequently the people most fanatically devoted to logic and

The alternative to mind is certainly madness. Our greatest blessings, says Socrates in the <u>Phaedrus</u>, come to us by way of madness—provided, he adds, that the madness comes from the god. Our real choice is between holy and unholy madness: open your eyes and look around you—madness is in the saddle anyhow. Freud is the measure of our unholy madness, as Nietzsche is the prophet of the holy madness, of Dionysus, the mad truth. Dionysus has returned to his native Thebes; mind—at the end of its tether—is another Pentheus, up a tree. Resisting madness can be the maddest way of being mad.

Norman O. Brown, "Apocalypse: The Place of Mystery in the Life of the Mind," *Harper's Magazine,* May 1961.

reason, to a cold review of the "facts" and a calculated construction of the truth, turn out not only to be terribly emotional in argumentation, but opinionated before any "truth" is "proved"—deeply committed to emotional positions that prove rock-resistible to the most massive accumulation of unsympathetic facts and proofs.

If man's mind cannot be turned into a logic-machine, neither can it function properly as a great emotional sponge, to be squeezed at will. All of us have known people who gush as a general response to life—who gush in seeing a sunset, who gush in reading a book, who gush in meeting a friend. They may seem to live by emotion alone, but their constant gushing is a disguise for absence of genuine feeling, a torrent rushing to fill a vacuum. It is not uncommon to find beneath the gush a cold, analytic mind that is astonishing in its meticulousness and ruthless in its calculation.

Somewhere between machine and sponge lies the reality of the mind—an amalgam of reason and emotion, of actuality and imagination, of fact and feeling. The entanglement is so complete, the mixture so thoroughly mixed, that it is probably impossible to achieve pure reason or pure emotion, at least for any sustained period of time.

It is probably best to assume that all our reasoning is alloyed with our emotional commitments and beliefs, all our thoughts colored by feelings that lie deep within our psyches. Moreover, it is probably best to assume that this stream of emotion is not a poison, not even a taint, but is a positive life-source, a stream of psychic energy that animates and vitalizes our entire thought process. The roots of reason are embedded in feelings—feelings that have formed and accumulated and developed over a lifetime of personality-shaping. These feelings are not a source of weakness but a resource of strength. They are not there for occasional using but are inescapable. To know what we think, we must know how we feel. It is feeling that shapes belief and forms opinion. It

Thought itself is engendered by motivation, i.e., by our desires and needs, our interests and emotions. Behind every thought there is an affective-volitional tendency, which holds the answer to the last "why" in the analysis of thinking. A true and full understanding of another's thought is possible only when we understand its affective-volitional basis.

L. S. Vygotsky, *Thought and Language,* 1962.

is feeling that directs the strategy of argument. It is our feelings, then, with which we must come to honorable terms.

Ideas and Experiments

1. Keep a journal of a writing project. Observe as closely as you can the processes you go through in order to start the language flow. Note the use of language to inspire thought—in particular, the jotting of disorderly or orderly thoughts down on paper. What would you advise someone with a writing block to do in order to get started?

2. What are some of the issues on which you have strong opinions? Write as logical a defense of that opinion as you can muster. Then delve deep within yourself and explore the roots of your belief. Are you able to discover the feelings (and their source) that have helped you shape the opinion? After deep exploration, are you anxious to qualify or modify your opinion?

3. Observe yourself in an argument or debate, noting your statements, and later analyze the basis for them—in reason or emotion, or some combination of these.

4. Listen closely to someone who claims to be talking about

facts, and speaking logically and reasonably. What are some of the possible emotional bases for the ideas he expresses?

5. Keep a diary of your linguistic involvements for a day. Analyze the occasions on which you spoke out with the voice of reason—but with a voice which you knew also came from deep feelings. Similarly explore the speeches of others. According to your observation, to what extent is language rooted in feelings, and to what extent in reason and logic?

Further Points of Departure

1. In his novel *Catch-22*, Joseph Heller presents his main character, Capt. Yossarian, desperately trying to find a way to get out of flying any more missions over enemy territory (in World War II). A new ruling has just decreed that anyone who is crazy will be grounded. The new rule has just been explained to Yossarian and he mulls it over (Orr is one of Yossarian's fellow Air Force officers):

There was only one catch and that was Catch-22, which specified that a concern for one's own safety in the face of dangers that were real and immediate was the process of a rational mind. Orr was crazy and could be grounded. All he had to do was ask; and as soon as he did, he would no longer be crazy and would have to fly more missions. Orr would be crazy to fly more missions and sane if he didn't, but if he was sane he had to fly them. If he flew them he was crazy and didn't have to; but if he didn't want to he was sane and had to. Yossarian was moved very deeply by the absolute simplicity of this clause of Catch-22 and let out a respectful whistle.[3]

3. Joseph Heller, *Catch-22* (New York: Simon & Schuster, 1961; rpt. New York: Dell Publishing Co., 1962), p. 47.

Many readers have believed that Joseph Heller, in *Catch-22*, has described the world as it really is. What do you think? (a) Read the novel and describe in some detail the nature of the Catch-22 world; (b) analyze the rational element in the paragraph quoted above, and relate it to the irrational; is there any ambiguity as to which is rational, which irrational? (c) write an account of one of your own experiences which demonstrates that this is, indeed, a Catch-22 world; (d) write a short story in which Catch-22 catches and holds all the characters (except, perhaps, the least aware).

3. Logic and Argument

As we become aware of the multilayered fabric of the soul, we try to ascertain not only the limits within which logical argument operates as a reliable tool, but also the areas in which that tool cannot be used, areas of different psychic dimensions. The laws of logic have colored philosophic thought ever since the Renaissance, especially since the seventeenth century. This influence is closely paralleled in the optical sphere by the influence of perspective on our view of the world. It is just these narrow criteria of logical cause and effect and of optical perspective that the present period resents and rebels against.

S. Giedion, "Symbolic Expression in Prehistory and in the
First High Civilizations," *Sign, Image, Symbol*, 1966.

Every day of our lives we find ourselves trying to figure something out systematically—arguing, being challenged to prove a statement, trying to behave *logically* in language. Most of us have, at some time or other, conceived the ideal rational life, in which all emotions are banned from the mind, all decisions made by reason, and all disputes settled by logic. And most of us have also, in the face of astounding experience, become disillusioned about the possibility of ever realizing the ideal rational life—of getting people to live by reason alone. Indeed, many of us have gone on to the conclusion that such a rational life would fail to be "ideal," and might even turn out to be nightmarish and anti-human.

The ways of logic have been pressed on us from time immemorial. One might reason inductively, by observing data or facts in enough particular instances to venture a justifiable generalization. Or one might reason deductively, beginning with a generalization that is widely accepted or taken for granted, and work back to a particular instance. And if those methods of reasoning don't seem relevant, one might try the syllogism, beginning with a major premise ("all men are mortal"), followed by a minor premise ("Socrates is a man"), and clinched by a conclusion ("therefore, Socrates is mortal"). The neatness and tidiness and simplicity of these methods have dazzled more than one young scholar. At first encounter they have often seemed the means to the creation of a utopia where reason might reign.

But seldom have a set of formulae disappointed so deeply. When one moves with these systems from the study to the street, a strange thing happens. The world seems indifferent to their classic simplicity, unamenable to their directness, and impatient with their irrelevance. No man has ever been known to decide which car to buy by the inductive method of investigation; no man has ever been known to decide which woman to marry by the deductive form of reasoning; and no man has ever been known to decide which presidential candidate to vote for through use of a series of syllogisms. If any has tried, the calculations may still be going on. Religious and political arguments are carried on hotly without reference to any forms of reason, and the man who tries to introduce them may have to run for his life. More frequently than not, the individual in an argument who repeatedly says, "Let's look at the facts," and who loudly insists on a logical analysis of the situation, is precisely the one individual most firmly committed to an emotional position, consciously or unconsciously. Age-old questions about God or the nature of reality remain largely untouched by all the "logic" that has been applied to them; and wars—supported on both sides by logicians and rationalists and "reasonable" men who use all the resources of their minds to "prove" the justness of their cause—continue to plague mankind.

The truth seems to be that man cannot live by reason alone, and even if some men could, the world at large would not permit it for long. But a deeper truth may well be that even if the world and all its inhabitants could be made to conform to some concep-

Reality, life, experience, concreteness, immediacy, use what word you will, exceeds our logic, overflows and surrounds it. If you like to employ words eulogistically, as most men do, and so encourage confusion, you may say that reality obeys a higher logic, or enjoys a higher rationality. But I think that even eulogistic words should be used rather to distinguish than to commingle meanings, so I prefer bluntly to call reality if not irrational then at least non-rational in its constitution—and by reality here I mean reality where things happen, all temporal reality without exception. I myself find no good warrant for even suspecting the existence of any reality of a higher denomination than that distributed and strung-along and flowing sort of reality which we finite beings swim in. That is the sort of reality given us, and that is the sort with which logic is so incommensurable. If there be any higher sort of reality—the "absolute," for example—that sort, by the confession of those who believe in it, is still less amenable to ordinary logic; it transcends logic and is therefore still less rational in the intellectualist sense, so it cannot help us to save our logic as an adequate definer and confiner of existence.

William James, *A Pluralistic Universe,* 1909.

tion of logic or reason, life in such a world really wouldn't be worth living because it would be devoid of common human satisfactions.

It is perhaps noteworthy that the human mind, the seat of that very logic that is seen by some as the panacea for all man's woes, has remained impervious to logical analysis, and remains as much a mystery as ever. But it now seems unlikely that logic and emotion are as separable as they once seemed. Basic to humanity is feeling—a complex of attitudes, emotions, and impulses representing the residue of a life's unique experiences of loving, hating, quarreling, winning, losing. This set of feelings, unique for each individual but with elements that are commonly shared, forms the major substance of motivation for all behavior, including the behavior of language, even the behavior of using language "reasonably" and "logically." Deep down, and determining, are feelings.

If such determining feelings are a condition of being human, there is no reason to lament the human lot. It is better to recognize the complexity and to work out a strategy that accounts for and exploits it. Even though it is impossible to be absolutely logical in all life's linguistic affairs, it is good to be reasonable. To be really reasonable would be to recognize the sometimes large, and nearly always hidden, part that feelings play in all uses of language.

Something of the nature of such reasonableness is suggested by Henry James in a passage from his essay, "Criticism," in which he attempted to explain the role of the critic. Although James was referring to the literary critic, his words may be taken universally as applying to all of us in our use of language in the "criticism" of life or experience—the use in which logic is so frequently demanded: "To lend himself, to project himself and steep himself, to feel and feel till he understands and to understand so well that he can say, to have perception at the pitch of passion and expression as embracing as the air, to be infinitely curious and incorrigibly patient, and yet plastic and inflammable and determinable, stooping to conquer and serving to direct—these are fine chances for an active mind. . . ." Here James recognizes that feeling is basic to understanding, that deep feeling leads to deeper understanding, to "perception at the pitch of passion." But such feeling does more than bestow depth of understanding; it provides the kind of understanding that leads to saying—in "expression as embracing as the air."

But there remains the question of prejudice, bias, wrongheadedness, feelings that might be perverse, bizarre, wrenched from common human paths. As everyone knows, the world is filled with wickedness—much of it based on feelings of hatred, of superiority, of pride, of self-importance, of holier-than-thou. However much we may at times doubt the universality of these traits, experience always seems to contrive to make us lose our doubts. And as we observe these traits manifest themselves in others again and again, the truth usually (but not always) and finally sinks in that we, too, are part of this universal scene—that we, too, on occasion exhibit these shocking traits. It is a wise man who knows himself. And to know oneself is to probe deeply down among the roots of opinions, to expose and bare to self-examination the hidden sources of bias and belief. Who can say what fears lie below prejudice, or what self-doubts reside within the strongest self-assertions. Perhaps the most fruitful research undertaken in assembling the materials for argument can be done within the depths of self.

In a kind of acknowledgment that everyday language is rooted in feeling, modern philosophy has come to recognize only one kind of logic as genuinely pure—symbolic logic, which uses nonword languages (purified symbols) for its concepts and proofs. But most men still feel that T. S. Eliot's Sweeney was expressing an aspect of the human condition when he exclaimed to his girlfriend Doris: "I gotta use words when I talk to you." Words seem inescapable, and their emotional involvement inevitable. Cynical

If certain scientific elements—concepts, theories, assertions, derivations, and the like—are to be analyzed logically, often the best procedure is to translate them into the symbolic language. In this language, in contrast to ordinary word-language, we have signs that are unambiguous and formulations that are exact: in this language, therefore, the purity and correctness of a derivation can be tested with greater ease and accuracy. A derivation is counted as pure when it utilizes no other presuppositions than those specifically enumerated. A derivation in a word-language often involves presuppositions which were not made explicitly, but which entered unnoticed.

Rudolph Carnap, *Introduction to Symbolic Logic*, 1958.

men will pretend otherwise, and will use language for manipulation while proclaiming their reason and logic. Honest men, on the other hand, will recognize the emotional source and impact of words, and will use language to explore and discover while acknowledging the limitations of words.

Argument ideally would consist of rational discussion among reasonable men, with full awareness of the dispersion of words in pools of feeling. Argument in fact consists of opposing strategies of linguistic wit, ingenuity, distortion, and even fraud. Despair of the first and contempt of the second of these approaches should not prevent the search for some kind of judicious balance between the two. No question felt deeply can be discussed void of emotion, but distortion can surely be minimized and fraud banned. Humane reason and aware wit are compatible resources in almost any human situation.

Ideas and Experiments

1. Write an account of a man who decides to use logic and

reason in selecting a woman to marry, a car to buy, or a politician to support.

2. Listen carefully to or read someone who claims to be using reason and logic in his discourse. Discover and discuss the role emotion plays in what he says.

3. How does feeling lead to understanding, in the Jamesian sense? Explore an instance you have observed, in yourself or someone else.

4. Put down on paper one of your pet prejudices or beliefs. After you have stated it simply, begin a process of self-probing to discover its origins, its nature, its consequences, and go as deep as you can in finding what lies underneath it.

Further Points of Departure

1. John Barth, in his novel *The Floating Opera* (1956), presents a character who attempts to live his life in accordance with pure reason. He formulates for himself a series of logical propositions formed on the basis of his analysis of the world and life:

> I. Nothing has intrinsic value. Things assume value only in terms of certain ends.
>
> II. The reasons for which people attribute value to things are always ultimately arbitrary. That is, the ends in terms of which things assume value are themselves ultimately irrational.
>
> III. There is, therefore, no ultimate "reason" for valuing anything.
>
> IV. Living is action in some form. There is no reason for action in any form.
>
> V. There is, then, no "reason" for living.

At a crucial moment in the novel, in the midst of his contemplating suicide, the character amends the last proposition as follows:

V. There is, then, no "reason" for living (or for suicide).[4]

By this amendment, he no longer attempts to do away with himself. You might try a number of responses to this set of propositions if they interest you: (a) read the novel and write an essay showing how they play a part in the work; (b) write your analysis of the propositions in the light of your own knowledge of the world and of life; (c) write a story in which a character tries, somewhat in similar fashion, to live his life by pure reason; work out for him a different series of propositions; (d) write a two-part poem in which the first part presents an individual on the point of suicide because of the reasoning above, and in which the second part brings the insight (in the amendment above) that makes the suicide unnecessary; the poem might be either serious or comic.

4. John Barth, *The Floating Opera* (New York: Appleton, 1956; rpt. New York: Avon Books, n. d.), pp. 238, 243, 270.

4. Beyond Logic

In the actual living of life there is no logic, for life is superior to logic. We imagine logic influences life, but in reality man is not a rational creature so much as we make him out; of course he reasons, but he does not act according to the result of his reasoning, pure and simple. There is something stronger than ratiocination. We may call it impulse, or instinct, or, more comprehensively, will. Where this will acts there is Zen, but if I am asked whether Zen is a philosophy of will, I rather hesitate to give an affirmative answer. Zen is to be explained, if at all explained it should be, rather dynamically than statically. When I raise the hand thus, there is Zen. But when I assert that I have raised the hand, Zen is no more there.

D. T. Suzuki, *Essays in Zen Buddhism: First Series,* 1911.

Mankind has been teased throughout history by sudden thoughts and flashes of insight that have appeared to be beyond reason and outside logic. Indeed, this form of mental phenomenon is so widespread and common that it must be taken into account in any description of the thinking process. It might well be argued that this kind of thinking—the surging forth of unsummoned ideas—is more important for writing than systematic concentration and laborious outlining.

It would be dangerous to habitually put off a writing task while waiting around for the flash of inspiration. This kind of postponement could develop into simply a weak procrastination, a cover for laziness. But there is something to be said for letting a subject or an idea or an attitude grow within before trying to present it in organized form on paper. We do this more frequently than we know, in all likelihood. And writers have probably always done it. In recalling the origin of one of his novels, Henry James wrote (in his Preface to *The American*): "I was charmed with my idea, which would take, however, much working out; and precisely because it had so much to give, I think, must I have dropped it for the time into the deep well of unconscious cerebration: not without the hope, doubtless, that it might eventually emerge from that reservoir, as one had already known the buried treasure to come to light, with a firm iridescent surface and a notable increase of weight."[5]

This "deep well of unconscious cerebration" is not a special but a common resource. We all have our "deep wells," and if we learn to use them they can become our richest source of material in the spinning out of words and ideas. If we reflect for a moment, we can remember some occasion in the past when we had a sudden revelation, a spontaneous insight that cleared away the fog and confusion surrounding a matter that had been troubling us. We might even be able to recall that these sudden insights

5. Henry James, *The Art of the Novel* (New York: Charles Scribner's Sons, 1934), pp. 22–23.

II. WRITING, THINKING, AND FEELING

But just as conscious contents can vanish into the unconscious, new contents, which have never yet been conscious, can arise from it. One may have an inkling, for instance, that something is on the point of breaking into consciousness—that "something is in the air," or that one "smells a rat." The discovery that the unconscious is no mere depository of the past, but is also full of germs of future psychic situations and ideas, led me to my own new approach to psychology. A great deal of controversial discussion has arisen around this point. But it is a fact that, in addition to memories from a long-distant conscious past, completely new thoughts and creative ideas can also present themselves from the unconscious—thoughts and ideas that have never been conscious before. They grow up from the dark depths of the mind like a lotus and form a most important part of the subliminal psyche.

We find this in everyday life, where dilemmas are sometimes solved by the most surprising new propositions; many artists, philosophers, and even scientists owe some of their best ideas to inspirations that appear suddenly from the unconscious. The ability to reach a rich vein of such material and to translate it effectively into philosophy, literature, music, or scientific discovery is one of the hallmarks of what is commonly called genius.

We can find clear proof of this fact in the history of science itself. For example, the French mathematician Poincaré and the chemist Kekulé owed important scientific discoveries (as they themselves admit) to sudden pictorial "revelations" from the unconscious. The so-called "mystical" experience of the French philosopher Descartes involved a similar sudden revelation in which he saw in a flash the "order of all sciences." The British author Robert Louis Stevenson had spent years looking for a story that would fit his "strong sense of man's double being," when the plot of Dr. Jekyll and Mr. Hyde was suddenly revealed to him in a dream.

Carl G. Jung, "Approaching the Unconscious,"
Man and His Symbols, 1964 (post.).

came at odd moments or in strange places, in contexts that apparently had nothing to do with their meaning or significance. They came and they established themselves by their sheer audacity and clarity, not by their appeal to logic. Their source in the reservoir of the unconscious, where they coalesced and exploded forth from the fluctuating amalgam of forgotten and unnoticed impressions, gave them weight and authenticity that commanded instant attention.

This experience is common enough to have inspired a vocabulary of its own—"hunch," "intuition," "impulse," "instinct." But whatever we call it, we all rely on it a good deal more than we usually admit to ourselves. We may tell others and even ourselves that we have reasoned through a problem and come to a conclusion or solution—when in fact we left the reasoning through to that "deep well of unconscious cerebration."

There is no reason why we cannot rely on a similar method for treating a subject on which we find we must—or want to—discourse. We may begin with a subject which leaves us cold, uninspired, uninvolved—one which lies in an unyielding lump as it is circled by our conscious mind; but if we, like James, drop it into our personal reservoir of cerebration, with a plan for future retrieval, we may discover that it will emerge not only with a "notable increase in weight" but even expanded (or narrowed) and divided into parts that have a natural relevance. The subject has become a specific topic, and we have discovered a point of view. We may begin, for instance, with patriotism and end up, on first retrieval, with some vivid feelings about treatment of the flag; with some notions about false patriots (who ostentatiously wave the flag), confused patriots (who mistake the flag for the country), and real patriots (who simply respect the flag); along with some vague emotions about the abuse and misuse of the flag, and some vague attitudes about the flag as symbol.

How is it possible that "patriotism," with a simple immersion in the reservoir, could gather to itself all this accretion? It came, no doubt, out of stored experiences and impressions that had been largely forgotten—and out of some that had passed unnoticed through the conscious directly into the unconscious, only to make themselves felt at times like these. If we should then, after some such experience, decide to launch forth on an essay on "patriotism," we might well look to the unconscious as a continuing resource—of minor and elaborative ideas, of details and extensions, of notions that need parenthetical insertion, and of notions that are in fact digressions, leading to other subjects, other topics.

Forget all rules, forget all restrictions, as to taste, as to what ought to be said, write for the pleasure of it—whether slowly or fast—every form of resistance to a complete release should be abandoned.

For today we know the meaning of depth, it is a primitive profundity of the personality that must be touched if what we do is to have it. The faculties, untied, proceed backward through the night of our unconscious past. It goes down to the ritualistic, amoral past of the race, to fetish, to dream, to wherever the "genius" of the particular writer finds itself able to go. . . .

The demonic power of the mind is its racial and individual past, it is the rhythmic ebb and flow of the mysterious life process and unless this is tapped by the writer nothing of moment can result.

William Carlos Williams, "How to Write," 1936.

No one has adequately described the mystery of writing, which is actually much less a continuous act of reason than an unpredictable series of spurts of "unconscious cerebration." Writing is in part like strolling in an uncharted woods, where we continually encounter unanticipated visitors, curiosities, distractions, obstructions. If these do not appear, turned up abundantly by the unconscious, our writing may move along—but be tiresome and dull in the end. However, if these elements surge up and take over the entire process of composition, our writing may clog and choke and sink in a bog of incoherence. What we must discipline ourselves to do is, first, to open our minds to this bubbling up from within, and, next, to pick and choose directions to go, ideas to follow, inspirations to pursue. And timing is important. There must be time for ideas dropped in the well of the unconscious to accumulate their weight, and they must not be left too long there for fear of dissolution. The time of actual writing must be a time of freshness if we are to rely on the surge of ideas to the surface of consciousness; fatigue stills the bubbling up from below, slows the mental actions and reactions generally. And after the act of writing, there must be a cooling-off time, a time for distance, even a time for forgetting, so that all the lapses that were overlooked or filled in the overflowing heat of composition will show their emptiness and command a renewed flow of thought.

Mastering the art of writing is not so much a matter of learning logic and following reason as it is recovering a sense of the mystery of the mind, a sense of the mystery that leads to respect. For centuries Western civilization has prided itself on its enlightenment through reason, a reason that has led to immense scientific achievement and to technological revolution. We have created an image of the ideal life as the life of reason, and we have worshipped logic.

What we have not frequently enough realized is that a large segment of the earth—the Orient—has another ideal, an ideal beyond reason, higher than logic. Zen Buddhism is but one manifestation of a general attitude in Oriental civilizations that elevates instinctive awareness to a level of reverence and awe. The question "What is Zen?" has elicited this reply:

Try if you wish. But Zen comes of itself. True Zen shows in everyday living, *consciousness* in action. More than any limited awareness, it opens every inner door to our infinite nature.

Instantly mind frees. How it frees! False Zen wracks brains as a fiction concocted by priests and salesmen to peddle their own wares.

Look at it this way, inside out and outside in: *consciousness* everywhere, inclusive, through you. Then you can't help living humbly, in wonder.[6]

Just as the West has attempted to make reason a way of life, with the ideal of the man of reason, so the Orient (and particularly Zen, but also other kinds of Buddhism) has attempted to make intuitive enlightenment a way of life, with the ideal of man *aware*. There is even, for Zen, a course of training that turns the mind away from logical and sequential thinking, concentrating on paradoxes and possible impossibilities—until there is a breakthrough to enlightenment.

Of course, such enlightenment and awareness are known in the West, especially by the poets (to name only three, Blake, Wordsworth, Whitman); and the Orient is not devoid of reason and logic. But the point is that there is something to be said for avoiding the extreme in either direction. We Westerners are more likely to find ourselves hung-up on logic than otherwise. And what we need to rediscover is the large part intuitive thinking plays in our use of language, and how much the richer we are for it.

Ideas and Experiments

1. Recall an important insight that came to you unsummoned. Reconstruct the incident with as much detail as you can recall, exploring the circumstances that may have brought about the insight.

6. Paul Reps, ed., *Zen Flesh, Zen Bones: A Collection of Zen and Pre-Zen Writings* (Rutland, Vt.: Charles E. Tuttle Co., 1957), p. 211.

2. Start with a subject that seems to leave you cold, something to which you do not immediately react. Drop it into your "deep well of unconscious cerebration" and pull it up periodically to see what has happened to it, particularly to see whether it has gained in weight. Think briefly about it, for example, before dropping off to sleep, and check the next day to see if there has been some accumulation. Write an account of your experiment—whether successful or not.

3. Contribute to the scanty knowledge about the writing process by observing the method by which you write. This can best be done perhaps by keeping a journal during the writing of an essay for some course other than English or for some purpose other than your English class. Try to write a complete biography of the essay, from the first idea to the last, with particular attention to the detailed ideas that came along the way—that filled in the outline. How did they come, where did they come from?

Further Points of Departure

1. Write a dramatic episode involving a man who attempts to live his life entirely by logic. The skit might be comic: perhaps the man is discussing with his girlfriend what they should do for the evening. Or it might be serious or bleak or absurd: a rational man trying to survive in an irrational world (perhaps he is repeatedly frustrated in some absurdly simple task—ordering a meal, driving a car, buying a book. . . .

2. Show how one of your favorite poets (Blake, Wordsworth, Whitman, Theodore Roethke, Allen Ginsberg, or some other) uses or exhibits nonlogical or Zen-like elements in his work. You might want to show how the poet creates a single poem out of an insight or a series of insights.

3. Use one of the following passages as an epigraph for a story

or essay suggested thematically by it (obviously, you'll have to let your imagination run a bit wild):

> I loafe and invite my soul,
> I lean and loafe at my ease observing a spear of summer
> grass.

(Walt Whitman, "Song of Myself")[7]

> To see a World in a Grain of Sand
> And a Heaven in a Wild Flower,
> Hold Infinity in the palm of your hand
> And Eternity in an hour.

(William Blake, "Auguries of Innocence")[8]

> To make a prairie it takes a clover and one bee,
> One clover, and a bee,
> And revery.
> The revery alone will do,
> If bees are few.

(Emily Dickinson, Poem 1755)[9]

> I walked on the banks of the tincan banana dock and sat down under the huge shade of a Southern Pacific locomotive to look at the sunset over the box house hills and cry.

7. Walt Whitman, *Complete Poetry and Selected Prose*, ed. James E. Miller, Jr. (Boston: Houghton Mifflin Co., 1959), p. 25.
8. William Blake, "Auguries of Innocence," *Poetry and Prose*, ed. Geoffrey Keynes (Bloomsbury: The Nonesuch Press, 1927), p. 118.
9. Emily Dickinson, *The Complete Poems of Emily Dickinson*, ed. Thomas H. Johnson (Boston: Little, Brown, 1960), p. 710.

Jack Kerouac sat beside me on a busted rusty iron pole, companion, we thought the same thoughts of the soul, bleak and blue and sad-eyed, surrounded by the gnarled steel roots of trees of machinery.

(Allen Ginsberg, "Sunflower Sutra")[10]

10. Allen Ginsberg, *Howl* (San Francisco: City Lights Books, 1956) p. 28.

II. WRITING, THINKING, AND FEELING

III. WRITING AND MEANING

1. How Language Means

My propositions serve as elucidations in the following way: anyone who understands me eventually recognizes them as nonsensical, when he has used them—as steps—to climb up beyond them. (He must, so to speak, throw away the ladder after he has climbed up it.)

He must transcend these propositions, and then he will see the world aright.

What we cannot speak about we must pass over in silence.

Ludwig Wittgenstein, *Tractatus Logico-Philosophicus,*
1921.

40. Let us first discuss this point of the argument: that a word has no meaning if nothing corresponds to it.—It is important to note that the word "meaning" is being used illicitly if it is used to signify the thing that "corresponds" to the word. That is to confound the meaning of a name with the bearer of the name. When Mr. N. N. dies one says that the bearer of the name dies, not that the meaning dies. And it would be nonsensical to say that, for if the name ceased to have meaning it would make no sense to say "Mr. N. N. is dead."

43. For a large class of cases—though not for all—in which we employ the word "meaning" it can be defined thus: the meaning of a word is its use in the language.

And the meaning of a name is sometimes explained by pointing to its bearer.

Ludwig Wittgenstein, *Philosophical Investigations,* 1953

There was a time when the meaning of language presented no problem, when it was a simple matter, upon being challenged as to meaning, to call to witness the dictionary. But in our age of universal skepticism, we have come to know that dictionaries are not depositories of eternal meanings of language. Dictionaries are made by ordinary human beings, who have collected data from—of all people—you and me, the general users of the language. Moreover, dictionaries simply hand back, in exchange for a word, more words—language for language. All this is not said to condemn dictionaries. They serve many purposes, but they do not solve the problem of meaning.

And the problem of meaning is the major philosophical problem of our time. In previous eras, philosophy accepted language as a primary means of apprehending reality. In our time, philosophy has challenged all language, and has devoted a major share of its time to the analysis of language, to the questioning of meaning, to discovering the meaning of meaning.

Among language philosophers, Ludwig Wittgenstein's name leads all the rest. Although it would be inappropriate, and even impossible, to present here a comprehensive explication of Wittgenstein's total body of philosophical writings, it is worthwhile to make a few observations about the direction of his thinking. What he went through in his monumental struggle to understand the nature of language and meaning might be duplicated by all of us on a smaller scale, and his experience might prove moderately helpful in moving us along in our understanding. For what he was concerned about has relevance for anyone attempting to work carefully with language, written or oral.

Wittgenstein (1889–1951) is the author of two important books, the first, *Tractatus Logico-Philosophicus,* published in 1921, and the second, *Philosophical Investigations,* published after his death in 1953. Both books have made a continuing

III. WRITING AND MEANING

impact on modern thought generally, and linguistic philosophy particularly. But the astonishing thing is that they represent two different directions in Wittgenstein's thought. In the first, he seemed to be calling for some kind of rigid adherence of language to the objects or facts of the world. One philosopher interprets him as saying: "If we are to think or speak at all, . . . there must be fundamental propositions owing their meaning and truth to their pictorial correspondence to states of affairs and facts respectively. . . . Sentences that do not express elementary, pictorial propositions are either collections, overt or concealed, of elementary propositions or they express no propositions at all and are devoid of meaning."[1]

As one might gather with this glimpse of the nature of Wittgenstein's early thought, most language of philosophy or of everyday use would be relegated, if his thinking were followed, to the mountainous heap of nonsense that was filling up the world. Language could get at truth, but only the truth of pictorial or physical reality, and only when controlled rigidly in relation to objects and facts. Wittgenstein concluded in the *Tractatus:* "The correct method in philosophy would really be the following: to say nothing except what can be said, i.e., propositions of natural science—and then, whenever someone else wanted to say something metaphysical, to demonstrate to him that he had failed to give a meaning to certain signs in his propositions. Although it would not be satisfying to the other person—he would not have the feeling that we are teaching him philosophy—*this* method would be the only strictly correct one."[2] Here Wittgenstein seems to be asserting that the only reality is the apprehendable, physical world; that discussion of the metaphysical, of the *nature* or first

1. A. M. Quinton, "Contemporary British Philosophy," *Wittgenstein: The Philosophical Investigations,* ed. by George Pitcher (New York: Anchor Books–Doubleday, 1966), p. 5.
2. Ludwig Wittgenstein, *Tractatus Logico-Philosophicus* (1921; rpt. New York: The Humanities Press, 1961), p. 151.

principles of reality, of the unseen, would be meaningless because there would be no physical or pictorial counterpart to the statements of that discussion. But he teased his readers by saying also: "There are, indeed, things that cannot be put into words. They *make themselves manifest.* They are what is mystical. . . . What we cannot speak about we must pass over in silence."[3]

If the world had been controlled by rules based on Ludwig Wittgenstein's *Tractatus,* there would have been a lot fewer words generated, a great many more periods of prolonged silence. But language has a way of escaping anyone's rules or laws; and human use of language has a way of continuing, even bubbling along, oblivious of philosophers' objections or advice. Moreover, Wittgenstein himself continued to follow uses of language not entirely approved in his *Tractatus,* and in his later *Philosophical Investigations* he made fundamental changes in his views. One interpreter writes: "Where the *Tractatus* saw language as a logically rigid essence concealed behind the contingent surface of everyday discourse, a skeleton to be excavated by penetrating analysis, in the *Investigations* language is accepted as it actually and observably is, as a living, unsystematic, and polymorphous array of working conventions for a large and not simply classifiable range of human purposes."[4] In the *Investigations* Wittgenstein abandoned his search for "meaning" in a rigid adherence between word and world, between language and observable objects and facts. Instead, he found the "meaning" of a word not outside the language but inside it, in its use—"The meaning of a word is its use in the language."

This much space has been devoted to Ludwig Wittgenstein's views because of the way they have shaped most modern thinking about language. Those of you who wish may pursue your interest by going directly to his books or by reading some of the more readily accessible followers who have embraced and elabo-

3. *Ibid.,* p. 151.
4. A. M. Quinton, *op. cit.,* p. 9.

III. WRITING AND MEANING

rated his views: Stuart Chase (*The Tyranny of Words*, 1938) or S. I. Hayakawa (*Language in Thought and Action*, 1949) or the periodical devoted to the field of semantics (symbols and their meaning), *Etc*. It is enough for our purposes here to note the modern quandary about meaning, and to reflect on how the problem relates to conventional advice to writers about avoiding vagueness of meaning, or striving for preciseness of meaning, or being exactly clear as to the meaning. Although there has been a revolution in modern philosophy centering on meaning in language, and although the simplest problems of meaning continue to puzzle and arouse fierce controversy, we often hear the platitudinous advice to "be precise," to "choose the exactly right word for your meaning."

Such precision and exactness, if it ever exists at all, is more likely to turn up in mathematical equations or chemical formulas. This is not to say that there can never be some kind of clarification of meaning by a shifting and changing of language. But it *is* to say that any suggestion that there can be an absolute precision or a final exactness in language is doomed to lead to frustration and disappointment. The equation or formula, reduced to an arrangement of precise symbols, has the character of the simple, prolonged sound of a pitch pipe, striking all ears with equivalent wavelengths of sound. A sentence in words, even of the simplest nature, has the character of a series of chords, offering a medley of sounds, vibrations, nuances and subtle combinations, unpredictable resonances—all sending out varying wavelengths of sound, striking different eardrums differently, and arousing different responses, some minor, others major. As other sentences are added, and paragraph piles on paragraph, the complexity multiplies geometrically, and countless reverberations sound and resound. Meaning in language conceived in this way is not, then, a matter of precision and exactness but a matter of resonance and reverberation, around, below, above, as well as in the words and linguistic structures.

1. HOW LANGUAGE MEANS   77

... psychic undertones differ from one person to another. Each of us receives any abstract or general notion in the context of the individual mind, and we therefore understand and apply it in our individual ways. When, in conversation, I use any such terms as "state," "money," "health," or "society," I assume that my listeners understand more or less the same thing I do. But the phrase "more or less" makes my point. Each word means something slightly different to each person, even among those who share the same cultural background. The reason for this variation is that a general notion is received into an individual context and therefore understood and applied in a slightly individual way. And the difference of meaning is naturally greatest when people have widely different social, political, religious, or psychological experiences.

Carl G. Jung, "Approaching the Unconscious,"
Man and His Symbols, 1964 (post.).

The primary reality of language rests not in the world of things and objects and facts, but in the minds of senders and receivers. Meaning is more a process of spinning possibilities than a process of delivering with machine-gun precision a staccato series of absolute realities or truths. Language does not prove—unless it is reduced to figures and symbols, and even then the proof will be more in the things, the objects, the realities, than in the symbolic representation. Language does not prove (the realities of the world), but it does persuade (the listener to believe); it does not change the world, but it does change listeners and readers; it does not affect the world, but it does move listeners to anger and joy, to agony and despair. In one sense, language seems powerless in its inability to manipulate objects of the world; in another sense, its power is awesome in its manipulation of the human psyche: it can give life (by instilling courage or a sense of self) and it can kill (by ridiculing, condemning, rejecting).

III. WRITING AND MEANING

Ideas and Experiments

1. Tune in on a serious conversation and discover how many times there occur in it misunderstandings of meaning. Follow up some of the instances and discover if you can what has caused the misunderstandings and what might have prevented them. Note any occasions in which some listeners misunderstood and others did not, or in which several interpretations emerged, none precisely coinciding with what the speaker thought he was saying. What are the causes? Write an account of your experiences and analyses.

2. Reread something you have written in the past, putting as much distance as possible between you and the piece of writing. Investigate the ambiguities that appear to you now that did not when you wrote the piece. How would you go about clearing them up? Try the piece out on some friends, and find out how they interpret it. Where there are differences between their interpretation and your intention, investigate the causes.

3. Write a short narrative, based on experience if possible, in which someone tried to make language do the impossible in changing the world. (Magic, incantation, curse.)

4. Write an account in which language did make a major difference in someone's life, either because he understood or misunderstood. In some cases, the language might have been spoken without thought, and the effect purely accidental—though no less serious for that.

5. Write two versions of a proposition in which you believe, one stripped down to essentials and couched in terms as precise and exact as possible; and another in which you exploit all the resonance of language in attempting to convey the complexity and subtlety of your proposition to your reader—perhaps even persuading him that the proposition is true.

Further Points of Departure

The following paragraph comes from Henry David Thoreau's "Civil Disobedience":

I have paid no poll-tax for six years. I was put into a jail once on this account, for one night; and, as I stood considering the walls of solid stone, two or three feet thick, the door of wood and iron, a foot thick, and the iron grating which strained the light, I could not help being struck with the foolishness of that institution which treated me as if I were mere flesh and blood and bones, to be locked up. I wondered that it should have concluded at length that this was the best use it could put me to, and had never thought to avail itself of my services in some way. I saw that, if there was a wall of stone between me and my townsmen, there was a still more difficult one to climb or break through, before they could get to be as free as I was. I did not for a moment feel confined, and the walls seemed a great waste of stone and mortar. I felt as if I alone of all my townsmen had paid my tax. They plainly did not know how to treat me, but behaved like persons who are underbred. In every threat and in every compliment there was a blunder; for they thought that my chief desire was to stand the other side of that stone wall. I could not but smile to see how industriously they locked the door on my meditations, which followed them out again without let or hindrance, and *they* were really all that was dangerous. As they could not reach me, they had resolved to punish my body; just as boys, if they cannot come at some person against whom they have a spite, will abuse his dog. I saw that the State was half-witted, that it was timid as a lone woman with her silver spoons, and that it did not know its friends from its foes, and I lost all my remaining respect for it, and pitied it.[5]

5. Henry David Thoreau, *The Variorum Civil Disobedience*, ed. Walter Harding (New York: Twayne Publishers, 1967), pp. 45–46.

III. WRITING AND MEANING

1. Write an essay exploring the meaning of freedom as it is defined by implication in this paragraph.

2. Read all of "Civil Disobedience," and discuss an aspect of the subject of freedom which interests you and with which you agree or disagree.

3. "I felt as if I alone of all my townsmen had paid my tax." Explore the meaning of "tax" as Thoreau uses it in this sentence, and write an essay on what it would mean, in this sense, to pay one's "tax" today.

4. Discuss the references to boys abusing a dog, and a "lone woman with her silver spoons." What is the meaning of these metaphors? How do they help Thoreau achieve the effect he desires? What other metaphors might he have used? How would they have changed the effect? (Could he, for example, have used metaphors of a cat abusing birds? a lone miser with his money?)

2. Words as Psychic Events

. . . the ideas with which we deal in our apparently disciplined waking life are by no means as precise as we like to believe. On the contrary, their meaning (and their emotional significance for us) becomes more imprecise the more closely we examine them. The reason for this is that anything we have heard or experienced can become subliminal—that is to say, can pass into the unconscious. And even what we retain in our conscious mind and can reproduce at will has acquired an unconscious undertone that will color the idea each time it is recalled. . . . Even the most carefully defined philosophical or mathematical concept, which we are sure does not contain more than we have put into it, is nevertheless more than we assume. It is a psychic event and as such partly unknowable. The very numbers you use in counting are more than you take them to be. They are at the same time mythological elements (for the Pythagoreans, they were even divine); but you are certainly unaware of this when you use numbers for a practical purpose.

Every concept in our conscious mind, in short, has its own psychic associations. While such associations may vary in intensity (according to the relative importance of the concept to our whole personality, or according to the other ideas and even complexes to which it is associated in our unconscious), they are capable of changing the "normal" character of that concept. It may even become something quite different as it drifts below the level of consciousness.

Carl G. Jung, "Approaching the Unconscious,"
Man and His Symbols, 1964 (post.).

Perhaps the best way of understanding the complexity of meaning that inheres in words and phrases and sentences is to view them as psychic events for both the speaker and hearer, the writer and reader. Words emerge from the depths of one mind, dripping with untold associations, shining with newly conceived intentions. They are sent out into the world and caught in another's delicate web and there plunged again into the depths of another mind, where there may be shock waves or stillnesses, depending on the receiver's psychic experience previous to this moment. Each word-plunge is a psychic event, unpredictable by the sender of the language. The shock waves that are started may reach long distances before they wear themselves out. As word follows word into the depths of a single mind, as the sequence of minor events merges to become a total happening, the shock waves bounce against each other, some cancelling, others reinforcing—until a totality of reaction coheres that is absolutely individual.

Psychic events are by their very nature, by the very nature of individual experience and individual minds, unique, differing radically from moment to moment in the same person, differing even more radically from individual to individual in a group or audience. Simple observation of some audiences will confirm this variation—some members are alert and puzzled, some are hostile and boo, some are warmed and applaud, some yawn, some sleep, some smile in aloofness, some stare in disapproval. But even this much identification and grouping is deceptive, because, of those who belong to any one group—those who boo, for example—all have experienced different psychic events, and have traveled quite different psychic paths to come together in a single moment of identical reaction. If we could retrace those paths we would be surprised at the differences that lie behind the momentary facade of sameness.

> **God in us: entheos: enthusiasm; this is the essence of the holy madness. In the fire of the holy madness even books lose their gravity, and let themselves go up into the flame: "Properly," says Ezra Pound, "we should read for power. Man reading should be man intensely alive. The book should be a ball of light in one's hand."**
> Norman O. Brown, "Apocalypse: The Place of Mystery in the Life of the Mind," *Harper's Magazine,* May 1961.

The act of reading is similar to the act of listening in an audience, in that both acts consist of sequences of psychic events. There are differences, of course. A member of the audience will be affected by the reactions of those around him and will find himself applauding or yawning without at first personally intending to; a reader will have the opportunity to reread and will not have visibly before him the actual writer to affect him in ways not connected with the language he uses. But in both cases—in all encounters with language—vibrations are set off deep within the mind and being, vibrations that are personal, intimate, and even irrational. The depth and nature of these vibrations are unpredictable and uncontrollable by the writer or sender of the words; they are often beyond the understanding and always beyond the control of the reader or receiver.

In short, language is full of mystery: indeed, full of a kind of magic. There was a time when man believed in the magic of language, when he used incantations to affect the course of events, when he cast spells and recited charms. Some remnants of that time are visible today in our public recitations of pledges of allegiance or in congregational prayers recited in unison. But as rational men we have all come to understand that language does not contain the kind of magic that can bring the spring rains for the crops or bring disease, destruction, and death to our enemies. In banning magic from language, though, modern man has too often failed to see that a good deal of mystery remains. Language is not the simple, rational system of communication that many would have us believe. Words do not remain simple bearers of messages, but rather explode into many fragments of meaning within each individual—and no one can foretell where the fragments may fly, what bruises they will leave, what flesh they will tear.

There is, then, in any concept of meaning in language, both a public and a private dimension. Regardless of how dominant the public or common meaning—language stripped to its bare essentials with "vibrations" held somehow to a minimum—the private meaning is always there to contend with, both on the part of the writer and the reader. And within the private meaning and

III. WRITING AND MEANING

the private response to language, there is always an element of the irrational.

The traditional concept of two kinds of meaning—*denotative* and *connotative*—figures in our understanding of this public and private dimension of language. The first of these terms has been defined as "the explicit meaning of a word," while the second has been defined as "the suggestive or associative meaning." For example, *politician* and *statesman* may have similar denotative meanings, but they have radically different connotative meanings: *politician* suggests an individual willing to deal in the dirty, compromising business of elective office, while *statesman* suggests an individual of principle, standing above dirt and compromise. But the important thing to note is that both these meanings, denotative and connotative, are public meanings—generally recognized and commonly understood when the words are used. There remains outside the denotative–connotative concept of meaning the whole, complex area of private meaning. For instance, the word *mother* means, denotatively, "the female parent," and means, connotatively, "tenderness, warmth, softness." But beyond these conventional and common meanings, each of us has an individual response to the word *mother* that has been conditioned by all our past experiences with a particular mother, and by observations of and encounters with other mothers. The individual response might be extremely complicated, beyond our own understanding, made up of both love and hatred, happy and unhappy experiences—or, in the case of an individual brought up in an orphanage, it might be a response compounded of anguish and bitterness. The psychic event of the word *mother* can be traumatic for some, pleasant for some, ambivalent for still others. The vibrations set off will reverberate and resound throughout the entire context in which the word appears. And other words will set off their own private vibrations, the total finally making up the private response to the private meaning.

In a sense, then, all language-use is a gamble and the best approach is to develop a strategy of calculated risk: the risk is always there, and it is best where possible to take it into account, to calculate it, and then proceed. If we took no risks, silence would reign supreme. However attractive that might sometimes seem, it would ultimately bring to an end our culture and our civilization.

Words in a poem, sounds in movement, rhythm in space, attempt to recapture personal meaning in personal time and space from out of the sights and sounds of a depersonalized, dehumanized world. They are bridgeheads into alien territory. They are acts of insurrection. Their source is from the Silence at the center of each of us. Wherever and whenever such a whorl of patterned sound or space is established in the external world, the power that it contains generates new lines of force whose effects are felt for centuries.

The creative breath "comes from a zone of man where man cannot descend, even if Virgil were to lead him, for Virgil would not go down there."

R. D. Laing, *The Politics of Experience*, 1967.

Most writers and readers recognize that this element of mystery or magic in language is the essence of poetry. The poet is always struggling, not to make new language, but to make language new: to capture surprise and wonder and mystery in new arrangements and new uses of words. He is critically dependent on this magic dimension, searching for the tone, the incantation, the chant that will set up the private vibrations deep within the readers. Emily Dickinson has described the poet thus:

This was a Poet—It is That
Distills amazing sense
From ordinary Meanings—
And Attar so immense

From the familiar species
That perished by the Door—
We wonder it was not Ourselves
Arrested it—before—.[6]

The poet has, in short, an acute awareness of the multitudinous private vibrations of language and deals with them, takes calculated risks with them, as a matter of course in the writing of poems.

But it must be remembered that the words of poems and the words of prose are all the same. The prose writer, too, often derives "amazing sense" from "ordinary Meanings." And the individual response to words and phrases is not likely to be affected much by whether the words come in set lines or in paragraphs. Whether producing poetry or prose, the writer takes calculated risks with the meanings of words. The keener his calculation, the more aware he is of the chance of remote vibrations, the more effective he is likely to be in accomplishing what he wants to accomplish.

Ideas and Experiments

1. Observe your language environment for a day or longer and collect a set of words that seem to be loaded with psychic repercussions, words to which people appear to react irrationally. Explore the causes for the variety of reactions to the words.

2. Observe yourself for a period of time and watch your private

6. Emily Dickinson, *The Complete Poems of Emily Dickinson*, ed. Thomas H. Johnson (Boston: Little, Brown, 1960), p. 215.

reaction to words. What words appear emotionally loaded to you? Can you trace back your experience with any of these words to determine part of the causes for your particular response?

3. "Your words are so loud that I cannot hear what you are trying to say." Explain this statement, and write a narrative in which this actually seems to be happening. You will probably want to present at least in part the interior story of the response to language, and you might need to use a special technique for presentation—perhaps stream-of-consciousness.

4. Find a poem that you like, and explore the general response to it as well as your own response. Can you discover in others or yourself private meanings or responses that enrich your experience of the poem? Or begin with a passage of prose.

5. Write a poem or short passage of prose and try it out on some friends. Ask them to tell you what they think it means. Pump them to find out whether they are revealing all their response to the piece. Then write an account of your experience (including the passage).

Further Points of Departure

The first chapter of *The Autobiography of Malcolm X* is entitled "Nightmare," and opens with the following paragraph:

When my mother was pregnant with me, she told me later, a party of hooded Ku Klux Klan riders galloped up to our home in Omaha, Nebraska, one night. Surrounding the house, brandishing their shotguns and rifles, they shouted for my father to come out. My mother went to the front door and opened it. Standing where they could see her pregnant condition, she told them that she was alone with her three small children, and that my father was away, preaching, in Milwaukee. The Klansmen shouted threats and warnings at her that we had better get out of town because "the good Christian white people" were not going to stand for my

III. WRITING AND MEANING

father's "spreading trouble" among the "good" Negroes of Omaha
with the "back to Africa" preachings of Marcus Garvey.[7]

1. Examine the passage for words, phrases, and references that
will evoke different feelings and emotions in different readers.

2. Read the entire opening chapter of *The Autobiography of
Malcolm X* and discuss the value of the writer opening the chapter as he did.

3. Write a "Nightmare" autobiographical chapter of your own
life, concentrating on the most horrifying or terrifying experience
you can recall. Write in such a way as to evoke a maximum of
sympathy from your readers.

4. Or if the experience in retrospect seems comic, write in such
a way as to evoke laughter.

5. Or if there is no horror or terror in your life, write an autobiographical chapter on how ordinary or banal it has been (and
show how the ordinariness or banality has its own kind of terror
—or comedy or tragedy).

7. Malcolm X, *The Autobiography of Malcolm X* (1965; rpt. New York:
Grove Press, Inc., 1966), p. 1.

3. *Language Games*

In opposition to this rationalistic view ["communication of thought
as the end of language"] I should like, for once in a way, to bring
into the field the opposite view: the genesis of language is not to be
sought in the prosaic, but in the poetic side of life; the source of
speech is not gloomy seriousness, but merry play and youthful
hilarity. And among the emotions which were most powerful in
eliciting outbursts of music and of song, love must be placed in the
front rank. To the feeling of love, which has left traces of its vast
influence on countless points in the evolution of organic nature, are

due not only, as Darwin has shown, the magnificent colours of birds and flowers, but also many of the things that fill us with joy in human life; it inspired many of the first songs, and through them was instrumental in bringing about human language.

Otto Jespersen, *Language: Its Nature, Development and Origin*, 1922.

> . . . what we are blind and deaf to within ourselves, we are also blind and deaf to in the outer world, whether it be playfulness, poetic feeling, aesthetic sensitivity, primary creativity, or the like.
>
> Abraham H. Maslow, "Isomorphic Interrelationships Between Knower and Known," *Sign, Image, Symbol*, 1966.

Language has been taken so seriously for so long that most people, when asked to consider it, relate it only to the sober side of life. Language performs serious functions in society: it provides the means for the communication of thought; and it is used for the burial and occasional resurrection of thought in large tomes that fill the shelves of libraries.

In fact, however, language is more closely allied to the playful side of life than the sober. And if we thought of it more in terms of love, of games, of dance, we would be entering more deeply into its spirit and essence. Even so traditional and distinguished a philologist as Otto Jespersen believed that the "genesis of language is not to be sought in the prosaic, but in the poetic side of life." Although he was thinking primarily of the origin of language in the beginnings of time, what he said seems to have considerable truth for the generation of language in everyday use.

III. WRITING AND MEANING

If we, in fact, kept an account of our language-use throughout a typical day, we would probably discover (unless we are super-serious people) that we use language more often for simple fun than for communication of serious ideas. We do, indeed, find ourselves more frequently on the poetic than on the prosaic side of life. We use language when we are at our ease in the sheer ebullience of good spirits—to express those good spirits—and thus create, unconsciously, poems in praise of existence. When we are feeling low, we use language to bemoan our own or the human fate, and curse the circumstances that have brought things to such an awful pass—and thus create unconsciously poems of dejection, darkness, or despair. We use language to gossip, and thus without pretension or consciousness create narratives, epics, myths which lighten our lives, amuse us or terrify us, or simply interest us and relieve the monotony of sustained, sober existence. We tell each other stories, jokes, anecdotes. We talk and we listen, we listen and we talk. And all the time we are snatching fragments from the flow of enigmatic human experience, reducing it to manageable form and understandable proportions.

> **This bondage to books compels us not to see with our own eyes; compels us to see with the eyes of the dead, with dead eyes. Whitman, likewise in a Transcendentalist sermon, says, "You shall no longer take things at second or third hand, nor look through the eyes of the dead, nor feed on the specters in books." There is a hex on us, the specters in books, the authority of the past; and to exorcise these ghosts is the great work of magical self-liberation.**
>
> Norman O. Brown, "Apocalypse: the Place of Mystery in the Life of the Mind," *Harper's Magazine,* May 1961.

In his later work (*Philosophical Investigations*), Ludwig Wittgenstein hit upon the analogy between language and games to suggest his complicated concept of the way language means. We might do well to adopt that analogy and look upon our various uses of language as playing a variety of games. The value of the analogy is that it reduces somewhat the seriousness with which we view the uses of language, emphasizes the fun and even the zest that we might find in language play, and suggests that just as there is an endless variety of games to play, so there is an infinite variety of language uses in which the rules change and shift. And just as games do not change the world, but do affect people (who might then change the world), so language has its effective meanings in the minds of individuals, not in things and objects. If I yell at the mountain to move, it will remain where it is. But if I enter into a language game with the people, and suggest—convincingly—that moving the mountain will beautify the landscape and bring wealth to the locality, I might bring about indirectly the move of the mountain. And the move might or might not produce the results I have suggested.

Doesn't the analogy between language and games throw light here? We can easily imagine people amusing themselves in a field by playing with a ball so as to start various existing games, but playing many without finishing them and in between throwing the ball aimlessly into the air, chasing one another with the ball and bombarding one another for a joke and so on. And now someone says: The whole time they are playing a ball-game and following definite rules at every throw.

And is there not also the case where we play and—make up the rules as we go along? And there is even one where we alter them —as we go along.

Ludwig Wittgenstein, *Philosophical Investigations*, 1953.

III. WRITING AND MEANING

But perhaps the most useful aspect of Wittgenstein's analogy between language and games is the suggestion of the variety that exists in language-uses and rules. We play one kind of game by ourselves when we throw the ball aimlessly and idly into the air without thought of regulations or rules—as we use language in reverie, in exploratory casting around for something to think about, in skimming over the day's events for moments of amusement in retrospect, all delightfully free of inhibitions and rules. In another kind of game, we encounter a gang of friends and begin throwing the ball about from one to another out of fun and exuberance, to see what might develop; just so, we toss out language constantly to friends and acquaintances, and catch the replies, in casual encounter and quick progression, without thought of conversation in depth until a remark or question brings a pause and prolonged exchange.

And what does language "mean" in these common uses? It means what its use indicates or says it means within the context of the use. What does a ball "mean" when we throw it idly to a friend in a group? It means that it attracts the attention of the friend, elicits a reaction (a catching) and response (throwing back). This may be all the "meaning" intended, wanted, or needed. Unstated are the assumptions: *I see you there, my friend, we exchange recognition, and we pass on.*

But of course Wittgenstein had in mind the application of the analogy of the game to *all* language use. When we are in the family, we play one kind of game, with one set of rules. When we live in a dormitory or boarding house, we play still another kind of game, with still another set of rules. And when we enter into law, or business, or education, or medicine, we play other language games with other rules. A dinner party of a selected group of people will be a special game that might develop its rules as it goes along, and even change them in the middle of the evening. Edward Albee's play *Who's Afraid of Virginia Woolf?* (played by two couples) illustrates this kind of dinner party game perfectly, as well as illustrating two private family language games.

And when we write, do we play a game? Not literally, of course; but we might well be better off for conceiving of any writing task as a kind of game in which we are devising some kind of strategy for winning, in the face of an opposition (readers) that must at every turn be taken into account. Of course, if we are playing a kind of solitaire, with only ourselves and our "cards" to consider—as in keeping a diary or writing a journal—then we need simply please, persuade, or move ourselves. But if there is an audience to contend with, it will largely determine the nature of the game and the rules that will apply—and set the "meaning" of the language used. Language that is relational—that is not confined to the individual but moves out to others—always finds its main meaning in that relationship. It is thus vital for a writer to find his principal strategies not only in the nature of his subject but also in the nature of his audience (as the participant in a game wins not only by analyzing the principles of play, but also in devising schemes to surprise his opponent).

The analogy of the game is most useful in suggesting the radical distortion that exists in the common concept of language as a means of communicating serious thought, as a product of pure reason or logic. If language is conceived as a game, the seriousness diminishes, the origin of language in playfulness and human feelings is emphasized, and the role of the imagination is restored to primacy.

A special kind of "game"—the dance—provides another analogy that might go even further in suggesting some other aspects of language. Since language arises from within as a kind of spontaneous response to existence, all utterance can be seen as a kind of verbal dance, a response to life and to other human beings. Just as some dances simply proclaim the individual's presence on earth, some utterances are sent forth simply to declare a presence, to pronounce, to affirm an arrival. Some dances involve two individuals moving around each other, together or apart, with grace and strength of movement. Conversations flow similarly, with meaning not so much in the individual words and phrases as in the ebb and flow, the movements backward and forward.

Even writing can be conceived as a kind of verbal dance. It is clearly a solo performance, and (it is hoped) reveals grace and strength. There is artistry involved in all the movements—there is the self to express, and the audience to reach. There is, perhaps, a choreography to follow, but the moment of performance will bring its own and spontaneous surprises. Or perhaps it is a modern dance, without a preconceived choreography, leaving to chance and impulse the precise directions and movements. It could have the character of a ballet, or of an Indian stomp dance, of an old-fashioned hoedown, or of modern rock and roll. But each individual puts his individual stamp on the style he follows. The dance arrests our attention, as does a piece of writing—by its impressiveness and its strategies. And as the dance "means," so does the piece of writing: both are human expressions that somehow command our attention.

Ideas and Experiments

1. How many games can you discover that you play with language? Select one that seems basically interesting, describe it, and write out the rules that seem to apply to it.

2. Select a piece of modern writing and analyze it in terms of a dance. What kind of dance does the piece suggest? How would you relate the various phrases and sentences to the movements of a dance?

3. Make up your own analogy for language-use—language as a "tool," as a "weapon," as a means of transportation, etc. Explore the usefulness (or absurdity) of the analogy.

4. Defend or attack the position that language is primarily a

means for the communicating of serious thought. Should one always attempt to speak from unemotional logic, from cold reason? Can one ever do so? (Use your own experience here in your argument.)

5. Defend or attack the position that it is frivolous to speak of language-use as a game. What are the elements of a game (or a dance) that have no counterparts in language-use? Do these tend to invalidate the analogy, and to distort the real nature of language?

Further Points of Departure

Write a story with one of the following sentences as an opener:

1. When she (he) slipped a note to me in class, asking if I understood the assignment, I knew the game had begun. I answered . . .

2. When my mother asked me if I had yet met the Smith's daughter (son), I could tell by the tone of her voice that there had been high-level discussions, and the game had begun. I answered . . .

3. Joe is my best friend. He is the kind of guy who always tells you what even your best friends won't tell you. On a late Friday night, when everybody is supposed to be out having a ball, he called me and caught me at home—because I had chosen to get some rest for a change. "Hey," he said, "have you heard what Marjorie said about you?" I knew the game had begun. I answered . . .

4. Walter is the nosiest boy in school, at least when it comes to grades. He can't stand not knowing what grade you got in a course, and he has elaborate schemes for ways of finding out. But the funny thing is, he always keeps his own grades secret. With him it is a game—to find out without telling. He always capitalizes on sympathy others have for him. He is not exactly a slob, but he is overweight and he always seems to be squeezing some

new pimple on his face. One time he came up to me after grades had been given out and used the ploy of a frontal attack. "Hey," he puffed (he always seems to be puffing), "you get your grades?" I knew the game had begun, and I knew he could do better than that. I answered . . .

5. As I settled in the aisle bus seat, I barely noticed who was sitting next to me by the window. But while I set about busily shoving a banged-up suitcase under the seat, folded my overcoat and placed it carefully in the overhead rack, and found my place in a paperback book that I have been reading on journeys for at least a hundred years, I felt a pair of eyes following my every move. I turned and found a little old lady smiling and nodding at me. "Well, young man," she said, "Is this your first bus trip?" I knew the game had begun. I answered . . .

You can no doubt beat any of these examples for openers. Make up your own account of a language game in your recent experience.

4. Making Language Mean

> "When I use a word," Humpty Dumpty said, in rather a scornful tone, "it means just what I choose it to mean—neither more nor less."
>
> "The question is," said Alice, "whether you can make words mean so many different things."
>
> "The question is," said Humpty Dumpty, "which is to be master— that's all."
>
> Lewis Carroll, *Through the Looking-Glass*, 1872.

The problem of meaning persists, and will no doubt continue to persist as long as language lasts; it is inherent in the nature of language. There will always be those who insist, in a literal-minded way, that words mean what the dictionary says they mean, nothing more and nothing less; and there will always be those who, like Humpty Dumpty in *Through the Looking-Glass*, insist that words mean whatever they choose them to mean.

As usual, the truth shuns extremity on either side, and takes a zigzag path down the middle, or near it. What do we mean by "meaning"? Books have been devoted to this question, but without divulging any universally affirmed answer. Words do acquire meaning through usage over the years, and these meanings do get collected in the dictionaries. But note that meaning accrues through usage, by the language-users like us, before it gets into the dictionary. The dictionary, then, is not a final authority—the final authority is the body of language-users. There is, if we look closely, irony in this circle. We language-users go to the dictionary seeking authority for the meaning of words, and we discover that the dictionary cites as its authority on the meaning of words the very language-users who consult it. How can this be?

This is simply one more example of a crazy, mixed-up world, full of the paradoxes that make life interesting. Language is in a constant state of change, and all that dictionaries can do is follow, not make change. The makers of change are the people themselves who use the language. When words change meaning (as many have radically changed throughout history, sometimes coming to mean the very opposite of their original meaning), it is because people begin to use words differently or with different meanings from the past, different from the dictionaries. How can they be understood when they strike out with new meanings? Clearly they cannot unless they provide contexts, or the occasions themselves or the social conditions provide contexts, that make the meanings clear and understandable.

All of us begin, then, with a heritage of meaningful language, and we are endowed with imaginations that can (and do) stretch, bend, and shift meaning. Collectively we make the language change and grow, and we then change the dictionaries. More than others, poets exploit this freedom to make language grow as a natural part of their professional creativity. Probably the most notable example of such exploitation is Lewis Carroll's "Jabberwocky":

> 'Twas brillig, and the slithy toves
> Did gyre and gimble in the wabe:
> All mimsy were the borogoves,
> And the mome raths outgrabe.
>
> Beware the Jabberwock, my son!
> The jaws that bite, the claws that catch!
> Beware the Jubjub bird, and shun
> The frumious Bandersnatch![8]

What Carroll has done is to keep basic structural patterns in order that his made-up words will be recognized as verbs or nouns, and he has brought together syllables from a variety of words that connote or suggest elements of meaning. It is quite easy, when reading "slithy toves," to conjure up in the imagination some nasty creatures that bear nightmare resemblances to "slimy toads." In a sense, Lewis Carroll is making words mean what he chooses to make them mean; but he is carefully taking into account elements of meaning (structure patterns, well-known syllables with residues of meaning) that the reader is ready to accept. The modern master of this technique is James Joyce, and his masterpiece in language creation is the novel *Finnegans Wake,* a massive book full of language distortion and invention.

Individuals can and do, then, make language mean, but they

8. Lewis Carroll, *Through the Looking-Glass* (1872; rpt. New York: Random House, 1946), p. 18.

are able to do so only with the assistance of conventions that are recognized and identified by their listeners and readers. Thus it can be said also that listeners and readers make language mean. They do so in the sense that they recognize the conventions used sufficiently to render new words or distortions meaningful for them. But they also make language mean in another sense—in the sense that their behavior will be affected by the way they interpret what they hear and what they read. This can be a total misinterpretation, or a misunderstanding, or a mistaken notion of the intention in speech or writing—but no matter, the reaction or behavior in response will be based on the assumed meaning— and that meaning will be as real for the receiver as the intended meaning was real for the sender.

A good example of speakers and listeners making language mean different things is seen in political confrontations, in which young college radicals whose life-styles are proclaimed by their long hair and casual dress yell obscenities at the police. As the obscenities hurtle through the air with greater volume and rapidity, the police (many of whom never had the chance to go to college and resent the hostility of the privileged people who do have the chance) become more and more tense and finally respond with clubbings and beatings, and sometimes gunfire. What does the language mean in a context of this kind? It is clear that among individuals of a certain life-style, obscenities are simply routine expressions of strong emotions, and evoke response in kind, but not violence. But the obscenities used outside this group (in which the language is understood and acceptable) can be interpreted as a deliberate provocation of violence. For the police who respond with clubs, the obscene phrases are literally "fighting words" which insult them and impugn their courage and honor. Many of them grew up in neighborhoods in which certain language aimed at an individual was intended to elicit the response, "Those are fightin' words," and to provoke a fight.

III. WRITING AND MEANING

Consider for a moment the obscenity "bullshit," a word which has largely lost its shock value because of its popular overuse. But as the word is commonly used today, it has very little connection with its original meaning of "barnyard manure." But there is enough residue of this meaning left for many to find the word extremely offensive. When one of the young radicals says to a fellow living the same life-style, "You're full of bullshit," they both understand the meaning (which is quite remote from the original) and the response is likely to be simply another obscenity. But when the young radical shouts this same sentence to a tense policeman, from an entirely different social background and group, the meaning *he* understands may be one remembered from his youth—"Let's fight, let's have it out to the end, you bastard." This is clearly a case in which the receiver of the language makes the language mean what he understands it to mean; and the meaning and understanding are powerful enough to evoke behavior based on that meaning—a response with a club or sometimes even a gun. The tragedy, as it sometimes turns out to be, cannot be averted by everybody turning to the dictionary as arbiter. The people involved would not in any case, and even if they did, the dictionary would not convince either party that the meanings they give the language are wrong. In a very real sense, both are making language mean, and are suffering the very real consequences.

This example of an incident of confrontation in the streets may be taken as a very crude and perhaps gross example of what happens in all language-use, including writing. The writer and reader together make language mean—and in the ideal situation they are making it mean the same thing—but often too they are not, not because of perversity or stupidity, but because of differences, like that between college radical and policeman. All of us are familiar with pieces of writing that have meant one thing to the writer, and a variety of things to his readers. This will probably always be the result to some extent with writing, particularly when it is long and complicated, subtle, rich in suggestion. But if a writer is going to approach the ideal of lucidity in meaning, he must immerse himself not in the dictionary but in language-use in many contexts, spoken and written, and he must develop a deep sensitivity to the nuances and subtleties of words and phrases. He must develop not only a strong sense of what he means and intends to mean, but he must also develop the imagination that enables him to foresee how readers will respond, not just to gross meaning but to the overtones and subvibrations of words.

Ideas and Experiments

1. Make a study of the "Jabberwocky" and write a twentieth-century poem modeled on it, but describing a nightmare city scene or something closer to your own experience. Can you write a modern "Jabberwocky" with political punch?

2. Write an essay or story in which you use a number of invented words and provide your reader the context for knowing their meaning without being specifically told what they mean.

3. Collect some examples from your personal experience of people (or yourself), making language mean something different from the generally accepted meaning. Or try out a few words or phrases and write an account of the reaction.

4. Find examples from the newspapers of incidents or clashes caused by senders and receivers making language mean different things. Reconstruct the incidents in an imaginative narrative.

5. Observe your own reaction to words, phrases, and sentences and give an account of instances in which you have made the language mean something different from the intention of the speaker or writer. Probe your background and discover, where you can, what caused you to bring a different meaning to the language than that which seemed to be intended.

Further Points of Departure

The following poem by E. E. Cummings can best be understood by reading it aloud:

anyone lived in a pretty how town

anyone lived in a pretty how town
(with up so floating many bells down)
spring summer autumn winter
he sang his didn't he danced his did.

Women and men(both little and small)
cared for anyone not at all
they sowed their isn't they reaped their same
sun moon stars rain

children guessed(but only a few
and down they forgot as up they grew
autumn winter spring summer)
that noone loved him more by more

when by now and tree by leaf
she laughed his joy she cried his grief
bird by snow and stir by still
anyone's any was all to her

someones married their everyones
laughed their cryings and did their dance
(sleep wake hope and then)they
said their nevers they slept their dream

stars rain sun moon
(and only the snow can begin to explain
how children are apt to forget to remember
with up so floating many bells down)

one day anyone died i guess
(and noone stooped to kiss his face)
busy folk buried them side by side
little by little and was by was

all by all and deep by deep
and more by more they dream their sleep
noone and anyone earth by april
wish by spirit and if by yes.

Women and men (both dong and ding)
summer autumn winter spring
reaped their sowing and went their came
sun moon stars rain[9]

1. Write an account of how the words in the poem take on meanings quite different from their dictionary definitions.

2. Write a narrative in prose presenting the full story of what is only implied in the poem.

3. Give an account of the visit that you have made recently to the graves of "anyone" and "noone," and describe especially your tour of the town where they lived, indicating what has happened to the town in the years since their death.

4. Can you do an urban version of the poem, putting "anyone" in a city apartment? Try using some of Cummings' strange and wonderful language, but introduce also some of your own. Per-

9. E. E. Cummings, *Poems 1923–1954* (New York: Harcourt Brace Jovanovich, 1940).

III. WRITING AND MEANING

haps you should introduce a new kind of cycle—*smoke, soot, sleet, slop.* Or: *haze, mist, fog, smog.* Of course, the language you introduce will determine the extent to which the poem turns ironic or comic.

5. Write a prose version of "anyone" and "noone" living out their life in the city.

PART TWO

THE WORLD IN WORDS

The second part of this book, the three chapters that follow, concentrates on the uses of language in the lives we live and in the worlds we inhabit. This part of the book is designed to develop an instinct for seizing on the possibilities of language in discovering the contours and hidden recesses of the inner worlds of the self; an agility for exploiting the potentialities and potencies of words in structuring the worlds without and beyond the self; and a capacity for projecting a *personal* voice into an impersonal void, as well as detecting the genuinely *human* voice in the generally dehumanized contemporary clamor. Although the focus is on the practical application of words to "reality," there is a hovering presence of the theoretical over all the discussions to suggest links and connections, rhythms and recurrences. A fundamental aim of this part of the book is to implant and nourish the power of the individual, to discover and to explore, to form and to shape, to create and re-create—both in work and in play—*the world in words*.

IV. WRITING AS DISCOVERY: INNER WORLDS

1. Discovering the Self

   . . . the mentality of mankind and the language of mankind created each other. If we like to assume the rise of language as a given fact, then it is not going too far to say that the souls of men are the gift from language to mankind.

   The account of the sixth day should be written, He gave them speech, and they became souls.

   Alfred North Whitehead, *Modes of Thought,* 1938.

. . . the fundamental human capacity is the capacity and the need for creative self-expression, for free control of all aspects of one's life and thought. One particularly crucial realization of this capacity is the creative use of language as a free instrument of thought and expression. Now having this view of human nature and human needs, one tries to think about the modes of social organization that would permit the freest and fullest development of the individual, of each individual's potentialities in whatever direction they might take, that would permit him to be fully human in the sense of having the greatest possible scope for his freedom and initiative.

   Noam Chomsky, "Linguistics and Politics—Interview," 1969.

"I speak; therefore I am."

Though this declaration may seem a little strange at first, it can be supported by considerable evidence. The individual establishes his individuality, his distinction as a human being, through language. He *becomes*—through language. Not only does he proclaim his existence, his being, through speech, but also his identity—the special and particular nature that makes him *him*. The declaration may then be rewritten: "I speak; *thus*, I am."

The creation of the self must, by its very nature, be a cooperative affair. The potentiality for language acquisition and language-use appears to be granted as a birthright. But the accident of birth will determine whether the language acquired will be Chinese, Swahili, Spanish, or English. And the same accident will determine the nature of the dialect acquired within the language. These "accidents" assume the presence of people and a culture that together bring the language to the individual.

If, then, the individual creates himself through language, it is only with the help provided by a sympathetic environment; a mother who encourages him to babble, to distinguish sounds and consequences, and then to utter sentences; and a host of other

It is language . . . that really reveals to man that world which is closer to him than any world of natural objects and touches his weal and woe more directly than physical nature. For it is language that makes his existence in a community possible; and only in society, in relation to a 'Thee,' can his subjectivity assert itself as a 'Me.'

Ernst Cassirer, *Language and Myth*, 1946.

people who act and react linguistically around him. Gradually as the individual develops, he acquires not only language but what might be called a "linguistic personality," a set of language behavior patterns that make up a substantial part of his identity as a person different from other persons.

This *creation of the self*—in the sense of the self's development into a distinctive person with distinctions that are in large part linguistic (or asserted or fulfilled through language)—is a creation of the self in a kind of gross or obvious sense. Few would quarrel with the rough outline sketched above, though some might want to express it in a different set of terms. But there is another, more subtle sense in which we can speak of the creation of the self implied in "I speak; therefore I am." This profounder sense is implied in Alfred North Whitehead's assertion that "it is not going too far to say that the souls of men are the gift from language to mankind." Where a nineteenth-century divine, or a twentieth-century philosopher, might refer to "souls," the modern psychologist might refer to the sense of an enduring self. This sense is generated, sustained, and preserved in language.

One way through which the sense of self is generated appears in the basic human impulse to sort through one's thoughts, or to think through the day's (or a lifetime's) experiences. To follow this impulse throws the individual back on his language resources. The experiences and thoughts that make up one's life are, in some sense, the essence of the individual, the things that are uniquely his and that make him what he is. In the process of sorting through his thoughts, or of disentangling and examining his tangled experiences, he is in effect defining himself, outlining himself, asserting and proclaiming himself. There can be no more vital activity for the individual: the results and the actions (new thoughts and new experiences) proceeding from it will further define his identity, not only for him but for the world he inhabits. In the old vocabulary, he is in this process revitalizing, reconstituting, refreshing, renewing his soul.

I did not exist to write poems, to preach or to paint, neither I nor anyone else. All of that was incidental. Each man had only one genuine vocation—to find the way to himself. He might end up as poet or madman, as prophet or criminal—that was not his affair, ultimately it was of no concern. His task was to discover his own destiny—not an arbitrary one—and live it out wholly and resolutely within himself. Everything else was only a would-be existence, an attempt at evasion, a flight back to the ideas of the masses, conformity and fear of one's own inwardness.

Hermann Hesse, *Demian*, 1925.

To live an aware life, the individual must begin with an awareness of self. He must conduct a running examination and periodic reexaminations of the self—in language, the medium of furthest reaches, deepest diving, most labyrinthine windings. The sorting through might well begin with the ordinary, everyday experiences of life. A diary or journal enables one to sift through and evaluate experiences, as well as to come to understand them and their significance—or insignificance. Most of us do this sifting and evaluation in moments of reverie or in that state of mental vagabondage just before sleep. There is some (even great) advantage, however, in subjecting ourselves to the discipline of written language, in which the vague and the mushy and the muddled must give way to the specific, the firm, the clearly formulated.

For writing *is* discovery. The language that never leaves our head is like colorful yarn, endlessly spun out multicolored threads dropping into a void, momentarily compacted, entangled, fascinating, elusive. We have glimpses that seem brilliant but quickly fade; we catch sight of images that tease us with connections and patterns that too-soon flow on; we hold in momentary view a comprehensive arrangement (insight) that dissolves rapidly and disappears.

Writing that is discovery forces the capturing, the retrieving, the bringing into focus these stray and random thoughts. Sifting through them, we make decisions that are as much about the self as about language. Indeed, writing is largely a process of choosing among alternatives from the images and thoughts of the endless flow, and this choosing is a matter of making up one's mind, and this making up one's mind becomes in effect the making up of one's self. In this way writing that is honest and genuine and serious (though not necessarily without humor or wit) constitutes the discovery of the self. It is not uncommon, before the choices are made, before the words are fixed on paper, to be quite unsure of which way the choices will go. Most people have experienced the phenomenon of their opinions or feelings changing, sometimes markedly, in the process of writing a paper which forces confrontations with language and choices among expressions. All people have experienced the clarification of their views and perspectives as they have worked through the process of placing them on paper. It is not at all unusual to find an individual who is uncertain and unclear about his feelings on a subject or an issue, but who, on discovering his attitude in the process of writing, becomes committed, often dedicated, and sometimes even fanatical: he has come to know himself. When this happens the individual is not being insincere, but is simply experiencing the discoveries of writing—discoveries that are often surprising and frequently exhilarating.

As suggested earlier, in setting forth on this voyage of self-discovery, it is best to begin, not with the problems of the universe, but with what appear to be the trivia of everyday events. Indeed, it might turn out ultimately that the big is somehow indirectly connected with the little. The self-examination which requires simply the writing of an account of one's life for a single day might bring unexpected illumination. Such an account would necessitate reviewing in detail and reliving imaginatively moments of pain and fun, joy and sobriety. A list of the events of that day (or week, month) would require consideration as to what, for an individual, constitutes events. Presumably they left some kind of mark—intellectual, emotional, imaginative. What kind of mark, how deep, how long-lasting? There might be public events and private events—events for which there were some, perhaps many, witnesses, and events that had no witnesses at all.

The list of a day's events in an individual's life might be posed against a list of the general public events and happenings—in the community, town, state, country, or world. Where do the two lists intersect, if at all? Did any of the world's events leave any mark on the individual, or did they reach him remotely or impersonally through the mass media, newspapers, radio-TV, and then fade into the distance? A third list might be composed of a close friend's perspective on the personal events on the first list, some of which he will have witnessed (but only externally), and others of which he will be totally unaware. Compilation of these lists, either in fact or imagination, may enable the individual to see the narrative of his life as marking a circle around him, with him—absolutely alone—at the center.

YEE-AH! I feel like part of the shadows that make company for me in this warm amigo darkness.
I am "My Majesty Piri Thomas," with a high on anything and like a stoned king, I gotta survey my kingdom.
I'm a skinny, dark-face, curly-haired, intense Porty-Ree-can—
Unsatisfied, hoping, and always reaching.

Piri Thomas, *Down These Mean Streets*, 1967.

This circle marks the individual's personal turf, material for his intellectual and imaginative use or growth that is his and his alone, impossible to share totally with anyone, no matter how close. One who begins to feel a sense of the preciousness of this material, this segment of life that is his and no one else's, is in fact feeling a sense of the self. If he begins to discover sequence and sense—a kind of unified narrative—in the events of his life for a day, he is making the discovery of self that the process of writing brings about: the unification must come from the individual's unique sensibility and identity.

Henry James had something of all this in mind in some advice he gave to young writers: "Oh, do something from your point of view; an ounce of example is worth a ton of generalities . . . do something with life. Any point of view is interesting that is a direct impression of life. You each have an impression colored by your individual conditions; make that into a picture, a picture framed by your own personal wisdom, your glimpse of the Ameri-

INTERVIEWER: Is there anything else you can say to beginning writers?

SIMENON: Writing is considered a profession, and I don't think it is a profession. I think that everyone who does not <u>need</u> to be a writer, who thinks he can do something else, ought to do something else. Writing is not a profession but a vocation of unhappiness. I don't think an artist can ever be happy.

INTERVIEWER: Why?

SIMENON: Because, first, I think that if a man has the urge to be an artist, it is because he needs to find himself. Every writer tries to find himself through his characters, through all his writing.

INTERVIEWER: He is writing for himself?

SIMENON: Yes. Certainly.

Georges Simenon, *Writers at Work: The Paris Review Interviews*, 1958.

can world. The field is vast for freedom, for study, for observation, for satire, for truth."[1]

Ideas and Experiments

1. Make a list of the events of your life for one day—say an average day—and construct a narrative of those events. Decide in the writing of your essay that your narrative will illustrate the meaningfulness of your life, the meaninglessness of your life, the tragedy of your life, the emptiness of your life, the absurdity of your life, or the nobility of your life; or perhaps will be emblematic of the belief that "all men live lives of quiet desperation."

2. Explore the ways that an important national or international event affects or does not affect your daily life. It might be that the event changes the course of your life, that it affects your life only in trivial ways, or that it actually becomes a kind of annoyance (however tragic it might be for some). It is possible, of course, that the only effect on you will be a sense of guilt for not feeling any effect.

3. Explore the nature of a small event that appeared big to you in the way it turned, or seemed to turn, the course of your life. Give an imaginative account of the effect of the event on others on the periphery of it—those whom it touched but did not similarly move.

4. Place yourself now on the periphery of an event which moves someone else deeply. Write an imaginative account of how the other person was moved, and how you were left relatively untouched.

5. Make an outline of your autobiography. What are the events to which you would devote chapters? What are the specific episodes that were crucial in making you what you are today? Write

1. Henry James, "A Letter to the Deerfield Summer School" (1889), *The Future of the Novel,* ed. Leon Edel (New York: Vintage–Random House, 1956), p. 29.

"A Chapter from my Autobiography." Concentrate on the change the events or incidents made in you and your life.

Further Points of Departure

In J. D. Salinger's *The Catcher in the Rye*[2] seventeen-year-old Holden Caulfield tells the story of the breakdown (or crack-up) of sixteen-year-old Holden in the greater wisdom of his accumulated year. Holden can look back on the critical events of his recent past with new awareness and understanding; but as he begins his autobiographical tale he makes clear that he is going to tell it in his own language and with his own sense of relevance. In the very opening sentence he states the terms and sets the tone in his personal voice, in such phrases as—"if you really want to hear about it" and "if you want to know the truth"—and he explains at the beginning that he is not going to present all the details of his childhood and "all that David Copperfield kind of crap," but is going to stick to the "madman stuff" that happened to him "around last Christmas." Thus Holden launches the story, in his unmistakable idiom, of the events that brought him to the psychiatrist's couch, from which he speaks to the reader.

1. Assume that you, like Holden, went through a crisis—spiritual, mental, physical—and write an account of it in which you give emphasis only to the "madman stuff" that happened to you that brought about the crisis. Do not, unless it is natural, assume Holden's voice. Use your own relaxed voice.

2. Read (or reread) *The Catcher in the Rye* and show how the seemingly unrelated episodes are related to Holden's state of soul.

3. If you have read (or now read) *Catcher in the Rye*, write your estimate of what Holden learns about his experience in the

2. J. D. Salinger, *The Catcher in the Rye* (Boston: Little, Brown, 1951; rpt. New York: Bantam Books, 1964), p. 1.

recounting of the experience. Pay close attention to the last chapter.

4. Write a character sketch of Holden from the point of view of Phoebe, or Mr. Antolini, or one of Holden's girlfriends.

5. Read *David Copperfield* or *Huckleberry Finn* and show how *Catcher* is different from—and also like—these other autobiographical, first-person novels.

2. *Versions of the Self*

Always know sometimes think its me
But you know I know and it's a dream
I think er no I mean er yes
But it's all wrong
That is I think I disagree

> John Lennon, "Strawberry Fields Forever," 1967.

I was trying to write . . . and I found the greatest difficulty, aside from knowing truly what you really felt, rather than what you were supposed to feel, and had been taught to feel, was to put down what really happened in action; what the actual things were which produced the emotion that you experienced. In writing for a newspaper you told what happened and, with one trick and another, you communicated the emotion aided by the element of timeliness which gives a certain emotion to any account of something that has happened on that day; but the real thing, the sequence of motion and fact which made the emotion and which would be as valid in a year or in ten years or, with luck and if you stated it purely enough, always, was beyond me and I was working very hard to try to get it.

> Ernest Hemingway, *Death in the Afternoon*, 1932.

Any serious examination of one's own life is likely to bog down in puzzlement before very long. Some of those questions that we like to put away without facing suddenly begin to surface. The external life is not all that difficult to comprehend—an act is an act, whether it be an embrace of love or a blow of hate; but the bafflement begins when we begin to wonder about the embrace of love that is mixed with hate, or the blow made with an agonized love. In short, when we begin to wonder about human motivation and human feelings, we lose our grip on the solid and observable, and begin of necessity to infer and speculate. To know the interior of another human being demands the keenest of imagination and the deepest of understanding. Because such knowledge is necessarily limited, though, to know ourselves —deep within our darkest and most distant corners—requires perhaps even greater reaches of will and effort: we tend to understand least that with which we live daily and intimately. Whitman has put the matter very well in a short poem: "When I Read the Book":

When I read the book, the biography famous,
And is this then (said I) what the author calls a man's life?
And so will some one when I am dead and gone write my life?
(As if any man really knew aught of my life,
Why even I myself I often think know little or nothing of my real
    life,
Only a few hints, a few diffused faint clews and indirections
I seek for my own use to trace out here.)[3]

We all, like Whitman have a "real life" within, which parallels but is by no means identical with our exterior life—our life of observable behavior and public acts. And it is probably true that if Whitman knew "little or nothing" of his real life, we likewise

3. Walt Whitman, *Complete Poetry and Selected Prose*, ed. James E. Miller, Jr. (Boston: Houghton Mifflin Co., 1959), p. 10.

know little of ours. If we are to come to know it, as we probably would like, simply because it is ours, we must follow the "few hints," the "few diffused faint clews and indirections" that we can find.

For some time now—I think since I was a child—
I have been possessed of the desire to put down the
stuff of my life. That is a commonplace impulse,
apparently, among persons of massive self-interest;
sooner or later we all do it. And, I am quite certain,
there is only one internal quarrel: how much of the
truth to tell? How much, how much, how much! It
is brutal, in sober uncompromising moments, to
reflect on the comedy of concern we all enact when
it comes to our precious images!

> Lorraine Hansberry, *To Be Young,*
> *Gifted and Black,* 1969.

There are no doubt many reasons for the difficulties in attaining self-knowledge, but one of the most common is the unconscious suppression of the self out of deference to social expectations. We are expected to feel certain kinds of emotions on certain kinds of occasions, and we develop the habit of expressing the emotions whether we feel them or not. Indeed, our habits so muddle up our feelings that we are unable to sort through them to know just how we do feel, just how we do react to an important event in our lives. The French writer Albert Camus, for instance, presents a character in *The Stranger* who is alienated from society because he is unable to feel and display the expected emotions on his mother's death. Ernest Hemingway pointed out, in fact, that one of the great problems of writing was in "knowing truly what you really felt, rather than what you were supposed to feel."

It is entirely possible that we have become so conditioned to hiding or suppressing our feelings that we can no longer find those that are really there, down deep below the ones that we pretend to have because society demands them. And indeed, it is possible that even after we have freed ourselves from exterior demands and pressures, we shall still find ourselves puzzled about our feelings and reactions. We may even find ourselves confronted with a number of possibilities and unable to choose because of the uncertainty of who and what we are, or want to be. We can, in short, be several selves, or none, or one. The self is never complete in its identity until life is over. During life it is always in process of becoming. We are creating it by the choices we make, the acts we take.

The self that lurks within deserves intimate acquaintance, even when it presents several faces, all enigmatic. For the struggling writer in search of sentences, this elusive, interior self pre-

Each man's life represents a road toward himself, an attempt at such a road, the intimation of a path. No man has ever been entirely and completely himself. Yet each one strives to become that—one in an awkward, the other in a more intelligent way, each as best he can. Each man carries the vestiges of his birth—the slime and egg-shells of his primeval past—with him to the end of his days. Some never become human, remaining frog, lizard, ant. Some are human above the waist, fish below. Each represents a gamble on the part of nature in creation of the human. We all share the same origin, our mothers; all of us come in at the same door. But each of us—experiments of the depths—strives toward his own destiny. We can understand one another; but each of us is able to interpret himself to himself alone.

Hermann Hesse, *Demian,* 1925.

2. VERSIONS OF THE SELF   121

sents some of the best material, and certainly the most exclusive —because it is inaccessible to anybody else. An individual's "outside" experiences are his alone, too; but they are frequently shared by others. "Inside" experiences constitute a private possession; no one can encroach, no one can borrow or steal or expropriate. Only the individual in possession can know this material, or come to understand it; and the deeper he goes, the richer his possession.

How deep, finally, can one go? As far as the imagination will allow. But surely to the level of biases, prejudices, hatreds, and hypocrisies. And perhaps to the fears beneath them. Normally we hide this darker self, even from ourselves. It is pushed down so far that it is difficult to penetrate to its depths. What is the point of raking through the muck, some might ask. There is, in fact, much point when it is the muck of one's own soul. Not because the pain becomes a pleasure, but because the pain might lead to understanding and illumination.

In these journeys into the darker self, it is well to plan a penetration in depth. Any human being is likely to find much within that is unpleasant, and difficult to admit as one's own. All of us, as a part of the condition of being human, have this nastier side, with inexplicable dislikes, blindnesses, hostilities. They flash out in our behavior, sometimes surprising even ourselves. But if we penetrate the lower depths, and search among the roots of these dark, evil flowers of the human spirit, we are likely to find their hidden sustenance in some kind of irrational fear. Penetrating bias and prejudice and hatred only to discover fear, we have come still nearer the center of the self. If we are able to come to some kind of terms with that fear, perhaps not to eradicate it (its roots might be so deep that they cannot be extricated) but to neutralize it through exposure and understanding, we can participate actively and directly and consciously in that creation of the self which is the major challenge of existence.

Life and literature are full of accounts of people who have tried to remake the world in their own noble image; they have been people (like Ahab in *Moby Dick*) who have had the loftiest of stated aims, the purest of proclaimed motives, the grandest of visible goals—but they have wrought havoc and destruction. And in their downfall they have frequently revealed their invisible and darkest selves as in sharp contrast with their proclaimed selves: they have acted from motives not nearly so pure and untainted as their followers or even they themselves have supposed.

It is clear, then, that the task of diving deep within oneself and finding what really lurks there is not an easy nor comfortable one, but it can be important, even definitive in the discovering of the self. And what will be uncovered cannot be predicted in advance. The deeper self is not necessarily the darker self. Muck is no more inevitable than sweetness and light, but there is likelihood of some unique and unsuspected mixture. Sorting through it, knowing it, and coming to terms with it is the job of a lifetime. And it is, finally, a job for language—the language of introspection, perhaps, but written language, too, in which the flow of inchoate feelings can be arrested, clearly delineated, and examined; and the sorting through can proceed in some kind of orderly fashion. Language cannot be a substitute for will, but it can present the case or basis for the will to assert its authority.

Finally, however, it must be admitted that there are interior spaces that cannot be penetrated, where no light can shine, and where no individual can enter. These are the spaces of darkness and silence, of terror, of ecstasy. Psychology speaks of these spaces as the unconscious. We can know the contents of our conscious mind, and we can penetrate it and bring it to some kind of order. But the unconscious is a mysterious province beyond our control and understanding. Sigmund Freud believed that it was a kind of sewer into which we dumped all the unhealthy and nasty elements of the conscious mind; D. H. Lawrence believed that it was a stream of primitive impulse marked by purity and health; Carl G. Jung believed that it was both private and "collective," connecting ultimately with a "racial unconscious" (a kind of universal unconscious of all men who ever lived), which became a source of mankind's archetypal myths. Others have asserted that there was no such thing as an unconscious, private or collective. But few men have denied that there are mysterious reaches of the mind beyond our understanding. And all men have agreed that we have glimpses into this mysterious realm in our dreams—the subject of the following section.

Ideas and Experiments

1. Begin an essay with the sentence: "I am the most fascinating character I know." Describe yourself as you think you really are, with all the depths that few people ever glimpse.

2. Robert Burns wrote in "To a Louse":

> Oh wad some Pow'r the giftie gie us
> To see oursels as others see us!

Try your hand at seeing yourself as others see you. Do a multiple self-portrait of yourself as you think you appear to a number of others—your mother, your brother, your closest friend, your most hated enemy, your teacher, or anyone else who may have a clear image of you. You might want to set the record straight by concluding with a portrait of the real you.

3. Make an exploration in depth of one of your prejudices or biases or pet peeves. If you think you don't have any, think again. Launch a voyage of self-discovery to find out if you really are as pure as you think. Once you have located a prejudice, and have faced up to having it, dig into its roots and find out what you

can of its hidden and deeper sources. Why does it grow and flourish? What might you do to eradicate it? Or do you think it is a virtue that should flourish?

4. Select an acquaintance or public figure, local or national, who is constantly proclaiming a righteous and noble point of view on some subject and explore the behavior of the individual in depth—as much depth as you can reach from your distance. Write a fictional narrative based on this individual in which you somehow dramatize the difference between the interior and exterior self.

5. What evidence do you have within *you* that you have or do not have an unconscious? Write a serious, or comic, account of a man who discovers his unconscious, falls into it accidentally, or suddenly realizes that he does *not* have one.

Further Points of Departure

A centuries-old philosophical debate has gone on about the essence of man's nature—divine or depraved? There have always been some who have argued that man is innately or naturally depraved, while others have maintained that he is pure and innocent, corrupted only by external social forces.

Perhaps if one aware and perceptive individual were to concentrate his gaze inward and, in total honesty, report to the world the nature of his own being, this old question could finally be cleared up.

Try your hand at being this individual. Retreat for a time from the world, meditate solely upon yourself at the deepest possible levels, and sort through with complete frankness your findings (which will likely be complex). Then write an essay maintaining—

1. Human nature is naturally depraved.

2. Human nature is naturally innocent.

3. Human nature is neither naturally depraved nor innocent, but . . .

4. The debate on the nature of human nature has been futile because . . .

During or after your experiment, you might want to look up two essays taking opposite sides of this question: Jonathan Edwards, "Sinners in the Hands of an Angry God"; and Ralph Waldo Emerson, "Self-Reliance."

3. Dreams: Windows on a Surrealist Self

The more that consciousness is influenced by prejudices, error, fantasies, and infantile wishes, the more the already existing gap will widen into a neurotic dissociation and lead to a more or less artificial life far removed from healthy instincts, nature, and truth. The general function of dreams is to try to restore our psychological balance by producing dream material that re-establishes, in a subtle way, the total psychic equilibrium. . . . Primitve man was much more governed by his instincts than are his "rational" modern descendants, who have learned to "control" themselves. In this civilizing process, we have increasingly divided our consciousness from the deeper instinctive strata of the human psyche, and even ultimately from the somatic basis of the psychic phenomenon. Fortunately, we have not lost these basic instinctive strata: they remain part of the unconscious, even though they may express themselves only in the form of dream images. These instinctive phenomena—one may not, incidentally, always recognize them for what they are, for their character is symbolic—play a vital part in what I have called the compensating function of dreams.

Carl G. Jung, "Approaching the Unconscious,"
Man and His Symbols, 1964 (post.).

And immediate experience of, in contrast to belief or faith in, a spiritual realm of demons, spirits, Powers, Dominions, Principalities, Seraphim and Cherubim, the Light, is even more remote [than experiencing the sensual world]. As domains of experience become more alien to us, we need greater and greater openmindedness even to conceive of their existence.

Many of us do not know, or even believe, that every night we enter zones of reality in which we forget our waking life as regularly as we forget our dreams when we awake.

R. D. Laing, *The Politics of Experience*, 1967.

Dreams have fascinated men from the beginning of time, in part because they remain basically fantastic and mysterious. The dream is, above all else, a private preserve. No one can truly possess another's dream. Moreover, even the individual who has had the dream finds difficulty in possessing it because dreams are often hard to remember. And even when possessed and held in the waking mind for examination, dreams frequently defy understanding. They seem to be made up of bizarre and incongruous elements, of fragments from various levels of time, of encounters that would be impossible in real life. Dreams are filled with both terror and ecstasy. Most of us have felt in our dreams the horrible sensation of falling or the pleasant sensation of flying. Most of us have been pursued by some grotesque creature that threatened our very lives, and some of us have felt the caress of some sensuous creature that promised ultimate fulfillment. We have felt embarrassment at suddenly appearing nude in front of an audience, or we have experienced the triumph of bringing an audience to its feet in wild applause. In short, we have had many experiences in our dreams that we have not had, and never could have, in real life.

Indeed, there is a surrealistic dimension in most dreams, with irrational juxtapositions, impossible events, weird landscapes: a symbolism that teases one with its hidden meanings and messages. Here is a recent dream of a contemporary man:

Driving along a road in a fast car, my brother in front and my wife (or is it my sister?) in back, I begin to feel unsure of the way and begin to look for landmarks and signs. I pick up the map and hold it out to my brother for him to check, and then I see the sign of the highway—147. Gradually the highway deteriorates and runs out completely. I come upon a car and swerve to the left, and run into a gulley and open land. The car bounces high several times, in a kind of slow motion. As it comes to rest, I look around to see what has happened to my wife and she is gone. I start looking for her, ask my brother, and then I start scratching the surface of the ground. The ground breaks through and there appears her head, and I scratch away the rest of the dirt above her: she has been buried beneath the ground but there are no signs that the sod has been broken or disturbed! I lift her up and hold her up by the waist, and she seems to be all right. Then she says that she wants a drink of water, and my brother says he wants one too. As we start to look for water, I wake up.

What this dream means is anybody's guess. Any serious attempt to interpret it would require first some discussion with the dreamer, who probably could provide several keys in his relationship with the people who appear in his dream, and in some account of his recent (and earlier) experiences.

Fiction writers have found the dream a rich source of reality, and have frequently used the dream to represent symbolically the situations or dilemmas of their characters. In *The Victim*, Saul Bellow portrays the victimization of Asa Leventhal one incredibly hot summer in New York by a forgotten acquaintance who unexpectedly turns up with the story that he has been the victim of Asa's carelessness, causing him (the acquaintance) to lose his job and even his sense of self-respect. In the midst of the nightmare confusion of victim and victimizer, Asa has a dream (at the opening of Chapter 14):

He slept but he did not rest. His heart beat swiftly and the emotions of the day still filled him. He had an unclear dream in which he held himself off like an unwilling spectator; yet it was he that did everything. He was in a railroad station, carrying a heavy suitcase, forcing his way with it through a crowd the sound of whose shuffling rose toward the flags hanging by the hundreds in the arches. He had missed his train, but the loudspeaker announced that a second section of it was leaving in three minutes. The gate was barely in sight; he could never reach it in time. There was a recoil of the crowd—the guards must have been pushing it back—and he found himself in a corridor which was freshly paved and plastered. It seemed to lead down to the tracks. "Maybe they've just opened this and I'm the first to find it," he thought. He began to run and suddenly came to a barrier, a movable frame resembling a sawhorse. Holding the suitcase before him, he pushed it aside. Two men stopped him. "You can't go through, I've got people working here," one of them said. He wore a business suit and a fedora, and he looked like a contractor. The other man was in overalls. "I must, I've got to get to the tracks," Leventhal said. "There's a gate upstairs. This isn't open to the public. Didn't you see the sign on the door? What door did you come through?" "I didn't come through any door," said Leventhal angrily. "This is an emergency; the train's leaving." The second man appeared to be a thoughtful, sympathetic person, but he was an employee and couldn't interfere. "You can't go back the way you came, either," the contractor told him. "There's a sign up there. You'll have to leave through here." Leventhal turned and a push on the shoulder sent him into an alley. His face was covered with tears. A few people noticed this, but he did not care about them.[4]

4. Saul Bellow, *The Victim* (New York: Vanguard, 1947; rpt. New York: Compass Books–Viking Press, 1956), pp. 168–69.

Although this dream has particular symbolic meaning for the protagonist of Bellow's novel, it nevertheless has the ring of familiarity for anyone who remembers his more frightening dreams—of seeking a way out of a maze, of being pursued, of looking for exits and entrances, of walking down endless corridors or tunnels, of falling through openings or off heights.

The world's literature is filled with the materials of dreams in which the dreamer-writers have often supplied some suggestions of meaning. In the seventeenth century Henry Vaughan wrote a poem called "The World" which opened:

> I saw eternity the other night
> Like a great ring of pure and endless light,
>   All calm as it was bright,
> And round beneath it, Time, in hours, days, years,
>   Driven by the spheres,
> Like a vast shadow moved, in which the world
>   And all her train were hurled.
> The doting lover in his quaintest strain
>   Did there complain;
> Near him, his lute, his fancy, and his flights,
>   Wit's sour delights,
> With gloves and knots, the silly snares of pleasure,
>   Yet his dear treasure,
> All scattered lay, while he his eyes did pour
>   Upon a flower.[5]

This is enough of the poem (it goes on for three more stanzas) to give some of its flavor. It is given to few people in their waking hours to see "eternity," and when anyone sees it in his dreams it is worth reporting to the world, even if the report is distorted or embroidered in the process.

5. Henry Vaughan, "The World," *Poetry and Selected Prose,* ed. L. C. Martin (London: Oxford University Press, 1963), p. 299. (The old spelling has been modernized for use here.)

The tone of Vaughan's poem, set by "pure and endless light" and "calm," gives the reader some reassurance about the nature of things. But George Gordon, Lord Byron's report of his dream (from the early nineteenth century), in a poem called "Darkness," gives no comfort at all.

> I had a dream, which was not all a dream.
> The bright sun was extinguished, and the stars
> Did wander darkling in the eternal space,
> Rayless, and pathless, and the icy earth
> Swung blind and blackening in the moonless air;
> Morn came and went—and came, and brought no day,
> And men forgot their passions in the dread
> Of this their desolation; and all hearts
> Were chilled into a selfish prayer for light:
> And they did live by watchfires—and the thrones,
> The palaces of crowned kings—the huts,
> The habitations of all things which dwell,
> Were burnt for beacons; cities were consumed,
> And men were gathered round their blazing homes
> To look once more into each other's face. . . .[6]

This poem goes on for many more lines, giving a bleaker and bleaker account of the end of the world—"The world was void,/ The populous and the powerful was a lump/Seasonless, herbless, treeless, manless, lifeless—/A lump of death—a chaos of hard clay." Byron had this dream—or at least something in the nature of a dream that served as the basis for this poem—back in 1816. The astonishing thing about it is that this is the twentieth century's waking nightmare—the vision of the world's end that has been made possible by twentieth-century inventions of destruction, or by the contemporary world's marked tendency to pollute

6. George Gordon, Lord Byron, *The Best of Byron* (New York: The Ronald Press, 1942), p. 149.

the earth, the waters, and the air, a pollution that if continued can only end in universal death.

One more report from the poets is presented here, this time in its entirety, to bring us back to the basic enigma and private symbolism of dreams. Critics have not yet come to any kind of agreement as to what Emily Dickinson's poem "In Winter in my Room" may mean, but they have all been fascinated by it and have found it important and successful:

> In Winter in my Room
> I came upon a Worm
> Pink lank and warm
> But as he was a worm
> And worms presume
> Not quite with him at home
> Secured him by a string
> To something neighboring
> And went along.
>
> A Trifle afterward
> A thing occurred
> I'd not believe it if I heard
> But state with creeping blood
> A snake with mottles rare
> Surveyed my chamber floor
> In feature as the worm before
> But ringed with power
> The very string with which
> I tied him—too
> When he was mean and new
> That string was there—
>
> I shrank—"How fair you are"!
> Propitiation's claw—

"Afraid" he hissed
"Of me?"
"No cordiality"—
He fathomed me—
Then to a Rhythm *Slim*
Secreted in his Form
As Patterns swim
Projected him.

That time I flew
Both eyes his way
Lest he pursue
Nor ever ceased to run
Till in a distant town
Towns on from mine
I set me down
This was a dream—[7]

Whatever the poem may mean symbolically, it makes a well-rounded narrative on its own terms, and Emily Dickinson no doubt realized this in setting it down. How much she herself understood the poem's symbols is hard to say, because she wrote in the late nineteenth century, in the age before Sigmund Freud and the advent of psychiatry and psychoanalysis. But even without explicit translation of the symbols, she may have realized that the poem communicated at the deeper levels of the mind.

Modern dream research has discovered a good deal about the general nature of dreams and the dreaming state. It has discovered, for example, that every sleeper has periodic stages of "rapid eye movement" during the night—periods during which the eyes move rapidly back and forth and in which other physiological signals indicate that the sleeper is dreaming. Sleepers who

7. Emily Dickinson, *The Complete Poems of Emily Dickinson*, ed. Thomas H. Johnson (Boston: Little, Brown, 1960), pp. 682–83.

have been awakened immediately after these periods have often been able to narrate complete dream sequences. It has been discovered also that dreaming periods are not instantaneous, as traditionally believed, but last around twenty minutes—about the length of time that the episode would require in actually happening. And it has been discovered that all people dream, and dream frequently throughout the night (rapid eye movement periods average around four per night): some people are better than others at remembering their dreams, but very few if any individuals remember all their dreams. Dreams are influenced by external events that take place during the dreaming period— loud sounds, for example, which are often simply incorporated in the story-line of the dreamer. Men in sleep experience penile erections that seem to coincide with the cycles of rapid eye movement, and which are not necessarily connected with erotic stimulus in the dream (so far as can be determined).

All this and more has been discovered by research that continues in many sleep-laboratories throughout the world, but it is unlikely that future discoveries will entirely clear up all the mysteries of our dreams. Although modern machinery can measure eye movement and brain waves and respiration and much more, it cannot enable the scientist to enter and observe the dream. He is entirely dependent on the memory and recall of the dreamer. This area of the self, of being, remains inaccessible to all except the dreamer. It may be the last private preserve left to man. With all its fantasy, the dream is some kind of message from the deepest self to the more clearly realized self.

Messages to the self that come from within should surely be heeded. The problem is in receiving and preserving them. At first, the problem may seem similar to that of looking for a message sent in a bottle via the ocean. But though not all the dreams will get through to consciousness, those that are rescued from oblivion are usually worth the effort.

And the effort requires both will and words. First there must

Unleashed from reason and detached from circumstance, the play of dreams is armed with terrible freedom. In all history and every recorded culture the mysterious and evanescent dream has been taken seriously. Strategic dream interpretations have altered the course of nations, as did Joseph with the fat kine and lean. Oracles dreamed the future. By pagan dream-rites the sick were healed. Lincoln's dream of death seemed a harbinger of his fate. American Indians enacted their dreams. During the reign of terror and superstition from the 12th through the 17th century, Western Europeans fought an international conspiracy of witches, and the seriousness of the dream was evident in the Malleus, guide and handbook to every judge of the Inquisition, at a time when dreams might mean burning. Dreams also inspired poetry in Coleridge, fiction in Robert Louis Stevenson, and Kekule, the organic chemist, is said to have deciphered the arrangement of atoms in the benzene ring by a dream of a snake eating its tail. The skillful man, said Emerson, reads his dreams for self-knowledge. Although dream books including codes for gamblers and advice on all aspects of practical life are abundant on newstands today, we tend to probe dreams for insight into the dreamer.

Current Research on Dreams, Public Health Service Publication No. 1389.

be the will to remember—and it must be exercised immediately after waking, before the dream has sunk so deep into the mind as to be virtually irretrievable. If memory succeeds in summoning the fast-fading dream back into view, words are required for retaining and understanding it—by first arranging it in comprehensible narrative sequence, and next by placing it down on paper in permanent form.

It is difficult to conceive of self-exploration that can be more interesting or exhilarating than deliberate contemplation of our own dreams. The dreams are interesting simply because of our own deep emotional involvement in them. Discovering some sense of their oblique meaning has all the excitement of breaking the code of a secret message. And the end of all the efforts is deeper self-understanding.

For the writer, self-understanding is justification enough for dream retrieval and dream exploration. For such self-understanding bestows awareness of and respect for the complexity of human behavior and human nature. It also bestows a healthy sense of mystery for the human mind and personality.

But a further benefit for the writer is that, by adding the dream world to his fund of interest and awareness, he increases considerably the creative resources at his command. He extends the areas and boundaries of his experience. He multiplies the ways he has of looking at events, at life, at the world. But he must begin by capturing his dreams in words (and they are often fascinating narratives just in themselves). And this effort will help him eventually in capturing—and structuring—reality in words.

Ideas and Experiments

1. Capture one of your own dreams and present it in narrative form. Can you supply any aspect of interpretation that only you could supply? (For example, were you eating an apple before going to bed to dream about apple trees?) How would you interpret the dream aside from the sources that you alone can trace?

2. Keep a diary of your dreams, and discover whether any pattern emerges. Write an account and an interpretation.

3. Borrow a dream from an acquaintance, friend, or relative and work out an interpretation. What is the reaction of the dreamer to your interpretation? How does your interpretation compare with his? Write an account of the experience.

4. How would you interpret the Emily Dickinson poem, "In

Winter in my Room"? You might want to look up something about her background, and check critical books on her to see how others have reacted to the poem.

5. Write a short story in which the dream told in the Emily Dickinson poem assumes an important role and which helps to explain the meaning of the symbolism of the poem.

6. Try casting one of your own dreams in the form of a poem; or use your dream as the basis for a poem, but, if you like, give more substance and form to the poem than the dream originally had.

Further Points of Departure

1. Read Saul Bellow's *The Victim,* and show how the dream of Asa Leventhal quoted above is related to his situation. Note another dream later in the novel (pp. 281–82): how does it relate to Asa's actual situation? Write an essay in which you show how Bellow uses the dream for fictional purposes.

2. Write a short story about an individual who appears to be trapped—physically or psychologically. Invent a dream or nightmare which represents symbolically his situation, and work it into the story.

3. The Russian writer Feodor Dostoevsky made extensive use of dreams in his fiction, and particularly in his most famous novel, *Crime and Punishment.* In this novel, the first of several dreams that haunt and torture the protagonist Raskolnikov appears in Part I, Chapter V, and carries him back to his youth, at the age of seven. Raskolnikov is a man who plots and carries out a terrible murder because he considers himself an extraordinary man above the laws of ordinary men. The dreams out of his unconscious appear to be messages of warning and alarm to his conscious self. Read *Crime and Punishment* and explore the meaning of Raskolnikov's dreams.

4. For medieval conceptions of dreams and their significance,

and for their use in fiction, see Geoffrey Chaucer's *The Canter-bury Tales*, "The Nun's Priest's Tale." Although this tale is ostensibly the story of Chanticleer the cock and his Lady Perte-lote, it contains a great many dream-stories told during the course of Chanticleer's discussion with his wives of his own fearful dream of a strange hound-like beast that tried to kill him.

4. The Ultimate Self

By knowing the Self . . . through hearing, reflection, and meditation, one comes to know all things. . . . As for water the one center is the ocean, as for touch the one center is the skin, as for smell the one center is the nose, as for taste the one center is the tongue, as for form the one center is the eyes, as for sound the one center is the ears, as for thought the one center is the mind, as for divine wisdom the one center is the heart—so for all beings the one center is the Self.

"Brihadaranyaka Upanishad," c. 500 B.C.

We are far more out of touch with even the nearest approaches of the infinite reaches of inner space than we now are with the reaches of outer space. We respect the voyager, the explorer, the climber, the space man. It makes far more sense to me as a valid project—indeed, as a desperately and urgently required project for our time—to explore the inner space and time of consciousness. Perhaps this is one of the few things that still make sense in our historical context. We are so out of touch with this realm that many people can now argue seriously that it does not exist. Small wonder that it is perilous indeed to explore such a lost realm. The situation

I am suggesting is precisely as though we all had almost total lack of any knowledge whatever of what we call the outer world. What would happen if some of us then started to see, hear, touch, smell, taste things? We would hardly be more confused than the person who first has vague intimations of, and then moves into, inner space and time.

R. D. Laing, *The Politics of Experience*, 1967.

Throughout the history of mankind, the idea has arisen again and again in religions and philosophies that knowledge of the self becomes, in some sense, the ultimate knowledge, the highest wisdom, attainable by man. The journey into the self is the most important journey any man can take: and he takes it by staying at home, withdrawing into his own being. In the middle of the nineteenth century, Walt Whitman began his journey this way (in "Song of Myself"):

I loafe and invite my soul,
I lean and loafe at my ease observing a spear of summer grass.
   . . . . .
Creeds and schools in abeyance,
Retiring back a while sufficed at what they are, but never forgotten,
I harbor for good or bad, I permit to speak at every hazard,
Nature without check with original energy.[8]

In the middle of the twentieth century, T. S. Eliot described the discovery of his journey in this way (in *Four Quartets*):

At the still point of the turning world. Neither flesh nor fleshless;
Neither from nor towards; at the still point, there the dance is,

8. Walt Whitman, *op. cit.* (above, n. 3), p. 25.

But neither arrest nor movement. And do not call it fixity,
Where past and future are gathered. Neither movement from nor
   towards,
Neither ascent nor decline. Except for the point, the still point,
There would be no dance, and there is only the dance.
I can only say, *there* we have been: but I cannot say where.
And I cannot say, how long, for that is to place it in time.[9]

In this impressive catalogue of paradoxes, Eliot is attempting
poetically to suggest the kind of knowledge that cannot be expressed explicitly in words—the knowledge that comes in the
ultimate encounter with the spiritual self. He says at the end of
Four Quartets:

> We shall not cease from exploration
> And the end of all our exploring
> Will be to arrive where we started
> And know the place for the first time.[10]

It is always the familiar that is hard to know. The self is so intimately familiar that it is hardest of all the aspects of life to come
to know in any profound sense.

Zen, it is said by Zen Buddhists, cannot be explained in words
directly. But a great many stories have been passed down from
the past, somewhat in the nature of anecdotes or parables, to
suggest the nature of Zen indirectly or obliquely. Here are two
from "101 Zen Stories":

18. A Parable

Buddha told a parable in a sutra:

A Man traveling across a field encountered a tiger. He fled, the
tiger after him. Coming to a precipice, he caught hold of the root

9. T. S. Eliot, "Four Quartets," *The Complete Poems and Plays* (New
York: Harcourt Brace Jovanovich, 1952), p. 119.
   10. *Ibid.,* p. 145.

of a wild vine and swung himself down over the edge. The tiger sniffed at him from above. Trembling, the man looked down to where, far below, another tiger was waiting to eat him. Only the vine sustained him.

Two mice, one white and one black, little by little started to gnaw away the vine. The man saw a luscious strawberry near him. Grasping the vine with one hand, he plucked the strawberry with the other. How sweet it tasted![11]

28. Open Your Own Treasure House

Daiju visited the master Basō in China. Basō asked: "What do you seek?"

"Enlightenment," replied Daiju.

"You have your own treasure house. Why do you search outside?" Basō asked.

Daiju inquired: "Where is my treasure house?"

Basō answered: "What you are asking is your treasure house."

Daiju was enlightened! Ever after he urged his friends: "Open your own treasure house and use those treasures."[12]

The paradoxes of Eliot's *Four Quartets* echo the paradoxes of these ancient Japanese tales of Zen. Each of the principal characters in the two Zen stories comes in some sense to know "for the first time" the "place" where they "started."

Henry David Thoreau, author of *Walden,* is famous for having traveled an immense distance by going only a short way away. He traveled out to the simple pond near his home town of Concord in 1845 and set up residence there for two years in a hut he built with his own hands, living largely off the produce of his own garden. He made clear his purpose in going to the pond when he wrote *Walden:* "I went to the woods because I wished to live

11. Paul Reps, ed., *Zen Flesh, Zen Bones: A Collection of Zen and Pre-Zen Writings* (Rutland, Vt.: Charles E. Tuttle Co., 1957), pp. 38–39.
12. *Ibid.,* p. 48.

Zen in its essence is the art of seeing into the nature of one's own being, and it points the way from bondage to freedom. By making us drink right from the fountain of life, it liberates us from all the yokes under which we finite beings are usually suffering in this world. We can say that Zen liberates all the energies properly and naturally stored in each of us, which are in ordinary circumstances cramped and distorted so that they find no adequate channel for activity.

This body of ours is something like an electric battery in which a mysterious power latently lies. . . . Zen . . . wants us to open a "third eye," as Buddhists call it, to the hitherto undreamed-of region shut away from us through our own ignorance. When the cloud of ignorance disappears, the infinity of the heavens is manifested, where we see for the first time into the nature of our own being. We now know the signification of life.

D. T. Suzuki, Essays in Zen Buddhism: First Series, 1911.

deliberately, to front only the essential facts of life, and see if I could not learn what it had to teach, and not, when I came to die, discover that I had not lived. I did not wish to live what was not life, living is so dear; nor did I wish to practice resignation, unless it was quite necessary. I wanted to live deep and suck out all the marrow of life, to live so sturdily and Spartan-like as to put to rout all that was not life, to cut a broad swath and shave close, to drive life into a corner, and reduce it to its lowest terms, and if it proved to be mean, why then to get the whole and genuine meanness of it, and publish its meanness to the world; or if it were sublime, to know it by experience, and be able to give a true account of it in my next excursion."[13] Like the man pursued by the tiger, Thoreau wanted to have lived before he died; and like the man seeking enlightenment, he turned his search toward his own "treasure house" within.

13. Henry David Thoreau, *Walden and Civil Disobedience,* ed. Owen Thomas (New York: W. W. Norton & Co., 1966), p. 61.

Whitman, Eliot, the characters in the Zen stories, Thoreau—all set off in quest of something we are all in quest of, what is sometimes called "the meaning of life," "the reason for being," "the purpose of existence." These terms may sound banal, and concern for them is sometimes brushed aside as sophomoric. But they somehow persist, and return to haunt even those who refuse to pay them heed. There is surely no man who ever lived who did not wonder, at some time during his life, what life was all about. Different men might well have phrased the question differently, and more sophisticated men might have disguised the simplicity and baldness of the question. But no matter how phrased, the question basically nags us all. The truth is, we answer the question for ourselves by the way we decide to live our lives. If we launch out on a ruthless pursuit of wealth or a mindless pursuit of pleasure, we have decided, consciously or unconsciously, what life is all about for us. Those who follow these paths are in some danger, perhaps, of suffering the fate that Thoreau was trying to escape—of discovering when it comes time to die that they have not lived.

Experience seems to be overwhelming that the ultimate answers to the ultimate questions must come from within. This is not to say that external experience does not contribute—whether it is being pursued by tigers or building for oneself a hut as a

> What is the aboriginal Self, on which a universal reliance may be grounded? . . . The inquiry leads us to that source, at once the essence of genius, of virtue, and of life, which we call Spontaneity or Instinct. We denote this primary wisdom as Intuition, whilst all later teachings are tuitions. In that deep force, the last fact behind which analysis cannot go, all things find their common origin.
> Ralph Waldo Emerson, "Self-Reliance," 1841.

retreat. Or, indeed, the reading of some books—*Walden,* or the Zen stories, or many another account of spiritual quest. But at the critical moment, one must confront the ultimate self for the definitive answer. If the knowledge of experience and the knowledge of books is not there transfigured into one's own insight, there is no genuine answer to the question.

We are constantly inquiring about the weather outside. More important is the weather within. Does calm prevail, or is there turbulence everywhere? How can we achieve the serenity, the equanimity, that enables us to "live deep and suck out all the marrow of life"? Each individual must somehow find his Walden pond, must plan his strategy for driving life into a corner to discover its nature and meaning, must work out his own encounter with his ultimate self. In this encounter, there is as much creation as discovery involved. The ultimate self that awaits our arrival within is shaped by us at the same time that it gives shape to our being and our lives. The encounter is likely to be an encounter surrounded by silences. But the nature of silence is such that it contributes—because it is the interval between its contrary, sounds. Language may not be able to contain the essence of the encounter, but it will be useful and even indispensable in making the preparation and in elaborating the consequences. Moreover, words can work wonderfully in oblique ways, as shown in the Zen stories about a philosophy that escapes the traps of all words. Finally, we can use language to deepen the silences.

Ideas and Experiments

1. Try out a contemplative session of your own, in which you "lean and loafe" at your ease and observe—a blade of grass, a stone, a fading photograph, a poster peeling off a wall, a modern superhighway cloverleaf, a smashed cigarette butt, or anything that happens to attract your attention within your personal range of vision.

2. How do you interpret the Zen parable of the man chased by the tiger? Write another parable in which you change the narrative but embody the same meaning.

3. Write a humorous or serious account of a man today who tries to find his Walden pond and follow the actions of Thoreau.

4. Everybody goes through a series of philosophies in the process of growing up. At stages they believe that they have figured everything out; but then the belief is undermined, a crisis follows, and the painstaking process goes on of constructing another belief. Look over your life and mark the stages of belief and the crises that followed. Write a spiritual autobiography, in which you examine these various stages and your behavior during the crises.

5. Do you have a credo now that you consider a kind of "enlightenment"? Can you put it into words? Or are you in pursuit of some meaning which you do not believe you have yet found? What are your plans for the pursuit? What would Thoreau do today? What would be a good plan for an individual who wanted today to find out some of the same things Thoreau said he wanted to find out? Work out a concrete sequence of actions.

6. Have you ever had what you might call an encounter with your ultimate self? Was it in some way mystical? Can you express what you learned in the encounter in words? Can you describe the circumstances of the experience?

Further Points of Departure

Dag Hammarskjöld writes in *Markings* (1964):

> Clad in this "self," the creation of irresponsible and ignorant persons, meaningless honors and catalogued acts —strapped into the strait jacket of the immediate.
>
> To step out of all this, and stand naked on the precipice of dawn—acceptable, invulnerable, free: in the Light, with the Light, of the Light. *Whole,* real in the Whole.

Out of myself as a stumbling block, into myself as fulfillment.[14]

This "marking" is one of a whole book of "markings" that appear to be gropings towards an understanding of basic as opposed to superficial values of life as it is lived. These markings are like the cryptic ancient runes found inscribed on stone tablets throughout Scandinavia.

Try your hand at keeping a book of "markings"—not a diary or journal, but a series of deeper thoughts jotted down as they come over a period of time. What are you able to discover about yourself—your real self—through your "markings"? Here is another entry from Hammarskjöld's *Markings:*

> What I ask for is absurd: that life shall have a meaning.
> What I strive for is impossible: that my life shall acquire a meaning.
> I dare not believe, I do not see how I shall ever be able to believe: that I am not alone.[15]

14. Dag Hammarskjöld, *Markings* (New York: Alfred A. Knopf, 1964), p. 152.
15. *Ibid.,* p. 86.

V. WRITING AS EXPLORATION: OUTER WORLDS

1. Encountering the World

It is not <u>how</u> things are in the world that is mystical, but <u>that</u> it exists.

Ludwig Wittgenstein, *Tractatus Logic-Philosophicus*, 1921.

Siddhartha learned something new on every step of his path, for the world was transformed and he was enthralled. He saw the sun rise over forest and mountains and set over the distant palm shore. At night he saw the stars in the heavens and the sickle-shaped moon floating like a boat in the blue. He saw trees, stars, animals, clouds, rainbows, rocks, weeds, flowers, brook and river, the sparkle of dew on bushes in the morning, distant high mountains blue and pale; birds sang, bees hummed, the wind blew gently across the rice fields. All this, colored and in a thousand different forms, had always been there. The sun and moon had always shone; the rivers had always flowed and the bees had hummed, but in previous times all this had been nothing to Siddhartha but a fleeting and illusive veil before his eyes, regarded with distrust, condemned to be disregarded and ostracized from the thoughts, because it was not reality, because reality lay on the other side of the visible. But now his eyes lingered on this side; he saw and recognized the visible and he sought his place in this world.

Hermann Hesse, *Siddhartha*, 1922.

Each self is the center of an ever-widening circle that expands to embrace the world and the universe. Each self is thus in some sense the center of the universe. If I would believe my own senses, the entire world was made to be arranged around me, to be apprehended by me. As I, the center, move through it, the circumference of my circle moves with me: I can never reach its edge. Moreover, the world is constantly changing through time. All the world's contents are either developing or decaying, changing and shifting and altering. Each day the world is a new world, waiting for me to rediscover it.

But there remains the exhilaration of first discovery. When we first looked out onto the world, and began to possess it by naming it, the excitement was difficult to contain. Rarely can we recall the intensity of the feelings of discovery, power, and creation that overflowed in us when we began as small children to move out into and take imaginative possession of the world. But if we observe children doing this, our old memories of initial encounter with the world are stirred. Most people continue to feel some sense of wonder as they walk out each day into the world—a world which either exhilarates, assaults, or brutalizes the senses, with views, sounds, odors, tastes, textures of infinite variety and grossness and subtlety.

Writers have always tried to preserve this sense of wonder at the world. Many poets have made wonder a part of the primary effect of their poetry, awakening in readers the old excitement of their youth. Here is Walt Whitman in "There Was a Child Went Forth":

There was a child went forth every day,
And the first object he look'd upon, that object he became,

And that object became part of him for the day or a certain part
   of the day,
Or for many years or stretching cycles of years.[1]

The poem continues with a catalogue of the world's contents
absorbed into the child—"early lilacs," "grass and white and red
morning-glories," "water-plants with their graceful flat heads,"
"friendly boys . . . and quarrelsome boys," "the old drunkard
staggering home," "all the changes of city and country wherever
he went"—all this and much more, says the poet, "became part of
that child who went forth every day, and who now goes, and will
always go forth every day."

   Although Whitman is speaking in metaphor, we do in some
sense "collect" the world as we move through it. We gather
impressions and store them away inside, there to mingle with our
being, to form some intimate part of us, to affect the way we
continue to see and encounter the world. This "collecting" of the

1. Walt Whitman, *Complete Poetry and Selected Prose*, ed. James E.
Miller, Jr. (Boston: Houghton Mifflin Co., 1959), pp. 258–59.

**By learning to name things a child does not simply add a list of
artificial signs to his previous knowledge of ready-made empirical
objects. He learns rather to form the concepts of those objects, to
come to terms with the objective world. . . . The first names of which
a child makes conscious use may be compared to a stick by the aid
of which a blind man gropes his way. And language, taken as a
whole, becomes the gateway to a new world. All progress here opens
a new perspective and widens and enriches our concrete experience. Eagerness and enthusiasm to talk do not originate in a mere
desire for learning or using names; they mark the desire for the
detection and conquest of an objective world.**

Ernst Cassirer, *An Essay on Man*, 1944.

world goes on from the moment of entering to the moment of departing. It is not peculiar to childhood—but children are perhaps more ebullient about the encounter, more delighted in gathering a great sweep of impressions, and more alive to and conscious of the impact on their lives and their interior being.

The key to this process is language. Without language, the world would remain one continuous blob of colors and shapes, inseparable and indistinguishable. With language it becomes classifiable and ordered and apprehendable. Children seem to know this instinctively. They want to know the names of things, not out of idle curiosity, but because the names have for them magical properties. By naming the object, by chanting the name over and over again, by skipping about the object while repeating its name, the object becomes imaginatively penetrated, delineated, possessed. In the entire process, the name is centrally important. And the name continues important in the imaginative life of the object within the individual. Sometime in the future, out of sight of the actual object, the naming of it again is an important part of its retrieval and retention.

It is a good deal easier for most people to state an abstract idea than to describe and thus re-create some object that they actually see. But the world of the fiction writer is full of matter, and this is what the beginning fiction writers are very loath to create. They are concerned primarily with unfleshed ideas and emotions. They are apt to be reformers and to want to write because they are possessed not by a story but by the bare bones of some abstract notion. They are conscious of problems, not of people, of questions and issues, not of the texture of existence, of case histories and of everything that has a sociological smack, instead of with all those concrete details of life that make actual the mystery of our position on earth.

Flannery O'Connor, *Mystery and Manners*, 1969 (post.).

We store an image of an object in our memory by its name; we summon the object from our memory by its name. Because we use their names, we are able to store innumerable images of objects, to build up a great storehouse and inventory of the world's contents. But even more important, because we have language, we can arrange and rearrange this inventory, placing objects first in one order and then in another: we link them, separate them, classify them, categorize them, and discover their relationships, differences, likenesses, individualities.

We all regret that we cannot retain throughout life the delight we felt as children in encountering and knowing the world. And we all have felt the impulse, in the face of the great flow of objects through the rush of time, to somehow stop the flow by rendering it in language, preserving it on a page. To snatch in language an object from space, or a moment from time, is to preserve in stasis something from the flux and flow. Language—written language—thus becomes indispensable in isolating and containing and preserving the pieces of our lives that strike us as meaningful. Language enables us to explore these pieces in depth and to reflect on them at length, giving us insight and understanding that would otherwise disappear in the ceaseless rush of experience.

The moment preserved, the object captured, may be on the surface astonishingly simple and seemingly trivial. The seventeen-syllable haiku of the Japanese serves the national imagination well in this regard. Almost every Japanese writes haiku, not because he considers himself a professional poet, but because the writing of these poems serves some personal need like that outlined above. Note the simplicity of these seventeenth-century haiku by the master, Bashō:

> How very cool it feels:
>   taking a noonday nap, to have
>   this wall against my heels.

On a journey, ill—
   and my dreams, on withered fields
   are wandering still.

With the scent of plums
   on the mountain road—suddenly,
   sunrise comes![2]

Here are some twentieth-century haiku:

In the withered fields
A horse-carriage whip sharply
Cracks against the sky.

                (Yamaguchi Seishi)

The sky is the blue
Of the world's beginning—from my wife
I accept an apple.

              (Nakamura Kusatao)

In the depths of the flames
I saw how a peony
Crumbles to pieces.

                (Katō Shūson)[3]

Haiku frequently present one image against another, often with
very little or no logical connection; and they present moments
that coalesce of their own accord, without plan or warning, striking a kind of minor key—outside the realm of "major" experience

2. Harold G. Henderson, *An Introduction to Haiku: An Anthology of Poems and Poets from Bashō to Shike* (New York: Doubleday and Co., Inc., 1958), pp. 29, 46.
3. Yamaguchi Seishi, Nakamura Kusatao, Katō Shūson, "Modern Haiku," *Modern Japanese Literature* (New York: Grove Press, 1956), pp. 381–82.

—that commands fleeting but intense attention. The apparent triviality of the objects or images, and the irrationality of their connection in a moment in time, all belie the depth of insight that is suggested. It is a historical fact that the haiku in its development is related to Zen and the Zen quest for enlightenment. More important here, the Japanese haiku is perhaps the best example around of the human compulsion and need to preserve in written language something of the ceaseless encounter with the world. And the preservation bestows an understanding that would otherwise escape in the flow of experience.

The fact is that our primary world of reality is a verbal one. Without words our imagination cannot retain distinct objects and their relations. . . .

The transformation of experience into concepts, not the elaboration of signals and symptoms, is the motive of language. Speech is through and through symbolic; and only sometimes signific. Attempt to trace it back entirely to the need of communication, neglecting the formulative, abstractive experience at the root of it, must land us in the sort of enigma that the problem of linguistic origins has long presented.

Susanne K. Langer, *Philosophy in a New Key*, 1951.

How is it that language has this magical property of not only providing a stasis in the midst of the continual flow, but of distilling an essence of meaning from a simple object or scene? It is the nature of language to symbolize, to abstract, to select, and it is the nature of the written language to contain, to frame, to salvage and save (the spoken language vanishes into air, the written endures). This nature enables language in the haiku (and elsewhere) to function as a magnifying glass, focusing the attention on fewer elements in greater intensity, and fixing the gaze on these elements in concentration and durance. The language thus not only frames the picture but invests the meaning; for the meaning is in the selection and juxtaposition, and is only latent (if there at all) in the jumble and disorder of the actuality.

Ideas and Experiments

1. Assume that you are, in the Whitmanian sense, a child "going forth" into the world. Make a catalogue of all the things you encounter on a long walk and show how they do or do not "become a part" of you. You might look up the rest of Whitman's poem and reflect on his total meaning and effect.

2. At a particular moment one day you pause, your attention caught suddenly by the way the sunlight reflects in a pool of rainwater, or the way a tire hisses as a car turns, or the way a half-torn letter is blown by the wind down a dirty street. Try your hand at distilling a moment like one of these into a haiku. (Be sure that you begin with one of *your* moments, and not a secondhand one like those above.)

3. Select an object—your desk, a tree, a lamp post, a statuette, a stairway, the entrance to a building—and concentrate your attention on it for some time until you feel that you have isolated it and imaginatively penetrated and outlined it, and then describe it in either a paragraph of prose or a poem, getting (as far as you can) the essence of the object.

4. Write an essay on the experience of doing 3 above. Analyze the language you have used and describe how it is selective, and how it invests meaning that was not necessarily obvious or clear in the original.

5. Recall a setting that on initial encounter was frightening or sinister, but which, on repeated encounters, became routine and boring. Capture if you can the original feelings and the nature of the setting that inspired them. Then show what the reality

turned out to be that changed the apprehension into boredom.

6. "But there is nothing to see," someone says. And you say, "Oh yes, there is if you open your eyes and look." "What?" is the inevitable reply. Tell him. You choose the place, taking into account the light at a particular time of day, and other factors that might change from time to time. Main street, the campus, the paths down by the pond or lake, a supermarket, a department store—there are innumerable places that could be freshly seen in this way.

Further Points of Departure

You might, if you start looking through a volume of Bashō's poetry, become a haiku-addict. There are worse fates for an aspiring writer.

1. Bashō wrote—

> Spring too, very soon!
> They are setting the scene for it—
> Plum tree and moon.

Write a prose description of the coming of spring; or write a haiku announcing the coming of winter, autumn, or summer.

2. Here are two other Bashō haiku:

> A sudden lightning gleam:
> off into the darkness goes
> the night heron's scream.

> Song of the cuckoo:
> in the grove of great bamboos,
> moonlight seeping through.[4]

4. Harold G. Henderson, *op. cit.,* pp. 42, 44, 47.

Explore the differences in effect of these two haiku, and show why the effects are different. Try your hand at a pair of contrasting haiku, and then explain how you deliberately created differing effects.

2. *Interweaving the World*

Perhaps the quickest way to understand the elements of what a novelist is doing is not to read, but to write; to make your own experiment with the dangers and difficulties of words. Recall, then, some event that has left a distinct impression on you—how at the corner of the street, perhaps, you passed two people talking. A tree shook; an electric light danced; the tone of the talk was comic, but also tragic; a whole vision, an entire conception, seemed contained in that moment.

But when you attempt to reconstruct it in words, you will find that it breaks into a thousand conflicting impressions. Some must be subdued; others emphasized; in the process you will lose, probably, all grasp upon the emotion itself.

Virginia Woolf, *The Second Common Reader*, 1932.

All life . . . comes back to the question of our speech, the medium through which we communicate with each other; for all life comes back to the question of our relations with each other. These relations are made possible, are registered, are verily constituted, by our speech, and are successful . . . in proportion as our speech is worthy of its great human and social function; is developed, delicate, flexible, rich—an adequate accomplished fact. The more it suggests and expresses the more we live by it—the more it promotes and enhances life. Its quality, its authenticity, its security, are hence supremely important for the general multifold opportunity, for the dignity and integrity, of our existence.

Henry James, *The Question of Our Speech*, 1905

After encounter with the world comes involvement and entanglement. In fact, they come simultaneously with the encounter. The individual finds himself on awakening to consciousness in an endless web of relationships, associations, groups, organizations, subcultures, and cultures. This web is spun with language, is held in place by language, is rent asunder and rewoven with language. As each individual is born into a world made up of the web, he too spins his web, creating new patterns of involvement: each individual spends his life interweaving the elements of his world into relationships and associations, largely with the stuff of language.

The role of language is made obvious in an organization that has a constitution, with bylaws, and rules of order. Here the written word becomes a kind of arbiter of behavior and justice—a fixed web that holds everything in its proper place. But language is just as binding in, say, a family unit, in which the "constitution" is unwritten, but rules generally are made clear, authority is established, methods of procedure and ways of conduct are understood—in language. Language has an authoritarian role, but it also has many other roles as used in the spinning of social webs. There is the delicate language of love—the "sweet nothings" that are really beyond expressible meaning; there is the language of hate—vituperative, obscene, raw, and coarse—meant to reduce or break a relationship; there is the language of polite and everyday social intercourse, language that holds the participants at a fixed social distance from each other that is comfortable for or at least acceptable by both—meant to maintain a relationship and not to tip it to one extreme or another.

In a basic sense we spin out our lives in language—creating the circles of our daily human involvements in language, as well as developing and establishing and bringing to fruition in it those involvements beyond our actual physical presence and ken.

We begin first at home (wherever we hang our hat, eat our dinner, and take our rest) with a family, either of the traditional kind or one made up of coequal elements, as in a dormitory or commune. Starting from this center there are ever-widening circles of social involvement. In the neighborhood there are casual and informal associations with those nearby—people with whom we discuss politics, taxes, street-cleaning, armchair philosophy, from whom we borrow a cup of flour and to whom we lend our charcoal grill. There is also a kind of neighborhood that moves with the individual, wherever he spends his time—at a job, in school, at a library: a circle of friends and acquaintances that form another linguistic web. And beyond the neighborhoods of the individual is the town or city, and beyond the city the county, and beyond the county the state, country, world, universe: ever-widening circles that contain the successive identifications of the individual, probably with weakening grasp and fading certainty. All of us come to view ourselves as living within some such hierarchy of structures as this, although we seldom stop to realize that these are linguistic structures of the mind, given order and pattern primarily by language. Who has ever seen the state or the world whole? But we know they exist because we hold the words that name them in our heads.

To me the converging objects of the universe perpetually flow,
All are written to me, and I must get what the writing means.
                                            Walt Whitman, "Song of Myself," 1855.

How much of our lives do we live in the space beyond our range of vision and in the time that lies outside the immediate now, in the past or future? In one sense, of course, we cannot live outside the physical space we occupy and the actual time that is present this moment. But—we constantly inhabit the space and time around and beyond, through imaginative projection of ourselves via language. We all are—in some degree—visionaries, historians, prophets, even though our frame of reference is limited to ourselves. We know or speculate on what lies beyond our personal sight; we have a conception of that past which casts us as the central figure and hero; and we have some conception of the future that will feel our presence.

This "knowledge" and these conceptions are all linguistic structures of the imagination. Indeed, without language our lives would soon shrink to primarily this space and this moment. Language enables the imagination not only to create structures outside the immediate realm of reality, but to give them a kind of permanence within the mind. The continuity of cause and effect, the interlocking sequences that we see in our past and project in our future, the patterns of intricately connected relationships that we see beyond our actual range of vision—these are products of the imagination in language created by us out of the actual flux and flow and confusion and chaos of all experience. The process of creation that we follow in establishing this continuity and these patterns is the same process of creation of the novelist and poet. Thus we are all creative artists of our lives, casting ourselves always in leading and frequently fascinating roles. We of course (most of us) do not publish our creation for the world. But we all frequently embody these imaginative creations in the spoken language, in gossip with our friends or discussions with our acquaintances. And we all also at some point commit to writing some aspects of these created continuities and patterns—in the writing of a diary, a journal, a speech, or in letters that are personal and professional or semipublic (to a newspaper, for example).

There is much to be said for becoming conscious where we are unconscious, for becoming aware where we are unaware. In other words, the continuities and patterns which we have spun out for ourselves might remain a muddle in our minds, or they might be spread out on a page and examined in the cold light of day. The

> Human civilization is an out-
> growth of language, and language
> is the product of advancing civil-
> ization. Freedom of thought is
> made possible by language: we
> are thereby released from com-
> plete bondage to the immediacies
> of mood and circumstance.
>
> Alfred North Whitehead,
> *Modes of Thought*, 1938.

very process of putting them on a page will reveal contradictions and impossibilities, and will force clarity. Language that floats around in the mind can remain comfortably vague, mushy, elusive, irresponsible. Language caught and fixed on a sheet of paper cannot be so irresponsible. There can, moreover, be genuine excitement in the creative process of working through the stage of the muddle in the mind to the stage of order and clarity on the page. There is always agony in writing, terror in confronting the whiteness of a blank sheet of paper; but the agony dissolves in exhilaration as a created thing takes shape on the page. The terror might cause flight; but it should be faced down, in the knowledge that the task when done will bring the deepest kind of satisfaction.

But satisfaction and exhilaration are not the only rewards from the struggle with writing out, creating on paper, the imaginative structures that one inevitably creates for his life. The process of writing can also immeasurably enhance the internal process of structure-creation and pattern-weaving. Writing can bring clarification (as for Eldridge Cleaver, who said, "[I write] to seek out the truth and unravel the snarled web of my motivation").[5] It can

5. Eldridge Cleaver, "On Becoming," *Soul on Ice* (New York: Dell Publishing Co., 1968), p. 15.

extend the vision, can explore the backward stretch of time in greater depth, probe the forward stretch of time with greater force. Writing can also bring the mind to focus for a sustained period of time on an area of life, a social structure, a segment of the past that existed heretofore only on the periphery of consciousness: and this sustained focus—a sifting and sorting and groping through language, a feeling of one's way along—can result in the creation of new structures, of new patterns that before existed only embryonically in the mind.

> **Words have users, but as well, users have words. And it is the users that establish the world's realities. Realities being those fantasies that control your immediate span of life. Usually they are not your own fantasies, i. e., they belong to governments, traditions, etc., which, it must be clear by now, can make for conflict with the singular human life all ways.**
> LeRoi Jones, "Expressive Language," *Home: Social Essays,* 1966.

We are all involved in interweaving our worlds—through imagination—in language. Indeed, the nature of our lives will be in large part determined by the way we interweave and create our world, and the consciousness with which we do it. We can live out our lives oblivious of the extent to which the reality we perceive "out there" is actually structured and patterned from within. But such a life lived unconsciously and unaware is empty of many exciting possibilities. On the other hand, the struggle of writing in explicit exploration of our created worlds pays off handsomely in new intensities of consciousness and awareness, in new dimensions of understanding and insight.

Ideas and Experiments

1. Read the epigraph by Virginia Woolf and make "your own experiment with the dangers and difficulties of words." Begin, as she suggests, with an event of some significance for you. After you have made your attempt, evaluate it in the light of the predictions made in her second paragraph—that, for example, in the process of writing you will probably lose "all grasp upon the emotion" felt in the actual event.

2. The epigraph by Henry James begins: "All life . . . comes back to the question of our speech." This is an extravagant claim. Explain insofar as you can what James means, and use your own "life" to examine the applicability of his point.

3. Speculate on the role of language in creating a reality for you that lies beyond your actual range of vision. You have, perhaps, a conception of Washington, D.C., without ever having been there. It is an entity with a shape in your imagination: how did it get there? How much did language contribute to the shape of the image?

4. Extract some sequence of events from the past and speculate on how those events may have appeared to participants (differently to different participants), how they have appeared in the reconstruction by those only on the edge of the action, and later by those who have come to know of the sequence only at second hand. You might use some historically insignificant events that took place in a community, or you might take a sequence of events that appears in the history books.

5. How much do you live your life in the future? Can you write a scenario—a fantasy, a satire, a prediction—for your future? Finish with a critique of the scenario, with some estimation of the chances of its actually being played out.

Further Points of Departure

In one of the notable modern American novels, Ralph Ellison's *Invisible Man* (1952), the hero (who remains nameless throughout the work) lives through a series of nightmare experiences in which other individuals attempt to use him and to thrust a ready-made identity on him. He resists, survives, and endures, and moreover, comes finally to a sense of self-awareness and self-identity: "And now all past humiliations became precious parts of my experience, and for the first time, leaning against that stone wall in the sweltering night, I began to accept my past and, as I accepted it, I felt memories welling up within me. It was as though I'd learned suddenly to look around corners; images of past humiliations flickered through my head and I saw that they were more than separate experiences. They were me; they defined me. I was my experiences and my experiences were me, and no blind men, no matter how powerful they became, even if they conquered the world, could take that, or change one single itch, taunt, laugh, cry, scar, ache, rage or pain of it."[6]

1. Are you able to look at your own life in the way that Ellison's Invisible Man is here looking at his? Write an account of your identity in the terms he uses to define himself here—your experiences, or your encounters with the world and the scars they left.

2. Compare the idea of identity contained in this passage from Ellison's *Invisible Man* with that contained in Whitman's "A Child Went Forth" (pp. 148–49).

6. Ralph Ellison, *Invisible Man* (New York: Random House, 1952; rpt. New York: Signet Books–New American Library, 1953), p. 439.

3. Read Ellison's *Invisible Man* and explore the ways in which his experiences gave him the identity he discovers at the end of the book—an identity different from any offered him or forced on him by individuals trying to use him.

3. *The Language of Media*

After three thousand years of explosion, by means of fragmentary and mechanical technologies, the Western world is imploding. During the mechanical ages we had extended our bodies in space. Today, after more than a century of electric technology, we have extended our central nervous system itself in a global embrace, abolishing both space and time as far as our planet is concerned. Rapidly, we approach the final phase of the extensions of man—the technological simulation of consciousness, when the creative process of knowing will be collectively and corporately extended to the whole of human society, much as we have already extended our senses and our nerves by the various media.

In a culture like ours, long accustomed to splitting and dividing all things as a means of control, it is sometimes a bit of a shock to be reminded that, in operational and practical fact, the medium is the message. This is merely to say that the personal and social consequences of any medium—that is, of any extension of ourselves—result from the new scale that is introduced into our affairs by each extension of ourselves, or by any new technology.

Marshall McLuhan, *Understanding Media:*
The Extensions of Man, 1964.

Motion pictures, the phonograph, radio, and television have all radically changed the way we live and the way we encounter the world. The movies deeply affected the theater, effectively killing the "popular" stage and leaving only a "legitimate" theater that is constantly struggling for survival. The phonograph, which made it possible to preserve musical performance and speech for an indefinite period, brought sounds and words into the home that previously could be heard only in large auditoriums with large audiences. The radio brought a "radio culture" of its own, constructed entirely on sound, and consisting of home-delivered music, drama, news coverage, political speeches, and much more. Most recently, television added picture to the sound, making it possible as never before to bring the entire world into the home —this in a literal sense after the launching of satellites around the earth that pick up signals from any part of the globe.

The marvels of these media are such as to confound the imagination, especially when it is realized that new developments will undoubtedly refine, extend, and improve these media. As one drives across the country, noting the ubiquity of the TV antenna, he is shocked into an awareness of how much the nation is held together in a correspondence of conformity by this medium. When he sees that people in New York and California laugh at the same jokes at the same time of day, that they hear the same political speeches, that they see the same news items of the most recent disaster, it becomes clear that the country has become homogeneous with a common culture as never before in history —this in spite of the fact that there are many more people spread out over greater geographical areas than ever before. It has, indeed, become possible for the first time in history for the world to become "one world"—technologically possible, that is.

But there are marvels beyond the unity possible with the mass media. Among the most important must be placed the journalistic possibilities. News from all over the world may be brought instantly into our homes, informing an entire populace, and on occasion an entire world, of events that may be occurring in some obscure, remote spot. The events, moreover, may be given a visual presentation that does much more than inform—it adds a dimension of reality that may evoke deep emotional response: tears at a natural disaster, fear at a criminal bombing, outrage at brutality. In addition to the news, discussion programs—presenting prominent people, politicians, professors, and just plain people—may examine important public and political issues of the day, informing, provoking thought, developing interest and awareness. Besides the journalistic possibilities are the marvelous imaginative and dramatic possibilities. More people have, in our time, witnessed a Shakespeare play, thanks to TV, than ever before in history. There have been original TV dramas and other programs of considerable merit—readings of poetry, presentations of ballets and symphonic orchestras, reruns of classic movies, performances by great tragedians, mimes, and clowns and many more.

This cornucopia of culture pouring into individual homes at the will of the home owner (and the price of a TV set) boggles the mind, especially when it is remembered that only a short time ago, as history counts time, men were primarily dependent for news and discussion on newspapers, magazines, and pamphlets; for drama and music on theaters and concert halls; and for serious ideas and fiction on books. Indeed, the shift from these media and forums to the current electronic media have caused some observers to proclaim the death of the printed langauge. They have pointed to the gradual disappearance of many of the familiar magazines, the reduction (sometimes by failure, sometimes by merger) of the numbers of newspapers in the big cities, the declining interest in fiction and the declining dependence on books generally for the needs now filled by radio and television. They then conclude that the printed word has become in some sense obsolete, and the book something of an anachronism.

But though the printed language has been pronounced dead by a number of contemporary pundits and prophets, it seems to have the curious capability of continuing in a dominant role in our culture. And one of the ironies of its doomsayers is that they have used the printed language as the means to proclaim its demise, very much like the character in *Moby Dick* who uses a light from the blubber of the whale in order to see to eat the meat of the whale. The very medium of the doomsayers is their message—the book lives on, and even those who pronounce it dead are dependent on its very life. Clearly the role of the written and printed language in our lives and our culture has been deeply affected by the new mass media—but it has not been displaced from the most significant functions it has always performed—functions of exploration, discovery, creation. The written language was performing these and other functions even before the invention of printing in the fifteenth century, and it will go on performing them as long as man remains dependent on language as the primary means of self-definition and the means of defining the distinctively human: in short, as long as man endures.

In spite of the mind-boggling possibilities of an electronic marvel like TV, the fact is that the programs that pour forth from it stupefy and stultify the mind. In the race to capture mammoth audiences in order to sell a sponsor's frequently unneeded and unwanted products, the quality of programs is aimed at the lowest common denominator of interest and intelligence. Canned programs with canned laughter fill up the time slots. It is not uncommon for a prospective viewer to turn from channel to channel on his TV set and finally give up in disgust because the programs are vacuous, empty, advertisement-ridden, innocuous, and stupid. TV has been called a wasteland, and many potential viewers would agree. There seems to be a poverty of intelligence and courage—alongside a crass commercialism—that reflects an image of our culture both repellent and discouraging.

But the greatest poverty of TV appears to be a poverty of the imagination. At one time in its history TV filled up its hours with quiz shows, without meaning or shape or creativity. Many of these continue. But even the dramatic shows which purport to present a play or story are devoid of imagination, with dialogue that has the ring of the phony, and with values that are weighted with the sentimental and romantic. And programs devoted to

America as Seen through the Eye of the TV Tube

1. Most people who work for a living (and they are few) are executives and/or work in some kind of office.
2. Sex is the basis of all psychological, economic, political, historical, social—in fact, known—problems of man.
3. Sex is very bad.
4. Sex is very good and the solution to all psychological, economic, political, historical, social—in fact, known—problems of man.
5. The present social order is here forever and this is the best of all possible worlds.
6. The present social order is here forever and this is the worst of all possible worlds.
7. The present social order is all in the mind.
8. Women are idiots.
9. Negroes do not exist. . . .

Lorraine Hansberry, *To Be Young, Gifted and Black,* 1969.

ideas or political debate too often turn out to be empty of ideas, remote from the real issues of the society, and slick performances aimed at basic emotional appeals—appeals to latent fears, hostilities, hatreds.

What has gone unnoticed, or at least unheeded, by the organization men of the electronic media, and by the prophets of doom for the printed page, is that any medium, no matter how marvelous in extending man's senses, is still dependent on man's imagination, and that imagination is dependent primarily on language, and that language finds its form and meaning and creative fulfillment in large part when it is committed to a page at some stage in its production.

But whatever the truth of the shortcomings of TV, it is true also that the electronic media have made major contributions to the country's culture and to its awareness of public and political issues. It is, perhaps, because TV's potential is so great that its failures are so disappointing. But it would be a mistake to sneer,

The mass media, together with radically improved storage and retrieval systems, have intensified the sense of an active synchronic present by keeping afloat in the public consciousness vast stores of information concerning past, present, and future previously available only to the few and after years of study. The media and the storage and retrieval systems have, of course, not supplied the reflection that converts mere information into understanding and makes it truly serviceable. But the instant science and neatly topical philosophy of the slicks combine with round-the-clock newscasts and stereotyped radio and television analyses to make the present weighty and momentous, and, at the peak of its own adolescent self-consciousness, youth understandably finds itself either intoxicated or terrified or both.
Walter J. Ong, "Crisis and Understanding in the Humanities," 1969.

as intellectuals once did, at the "boob-tube," and to decry its development. The electronic media have changed our way of life and have expanded our awareness of the world. Individuals who grow up with TV know more about the world and their place in it than those who grew up without it. TV culture should not be condemned as inferior to book culture, nor should it be hailed as replacing the printed word. The two cultures are, in fact, quite interdependent, both drawing (at their best) on common sources of the imagination and language, each at its best reinforcing the other—uniting to help shape human understanding and awareness.

Ideas and Experiments

1. In the epigraph Marshall McLuhan says "the medium is the message." Explore the meaning and ramifications and implications of this statement.

2. Write an account of the impact of the phonograph (and tape recorder) on modern music. Explore the ways in which the

means (or media) have shaped the substance—the music. You probably should begin this project only if you already have a fairly wide acquaintance with modern music of various kinds, including electronic.

3. Watch TV for a day without cease, making notes along the way, and write a critique of the programming. Be sure to keep an open mind, and tell what is good as well as what is bad.

4. Observe a daily news program on TV for a period of a week and write an account of the impact of the program and how it is achieved. Explore the editorial point of view manifested in the selections of news items, the method of reporting them, and the selection of pictures. It has been said that a picture is worth a thousand words (or more). Is this saying borne out by TV news presentation?

5. Evaluate the quality of one of the talk-shows that appear late at night (and sometimes during the day). Or evaluate the level of discussion of ideas on one of the interview shows in which a public figure responds to questions.

6. If you have an educational station in your community, watch it for a period of time and make a critique of its successes and failures.

7. All TV and radio stations are supposed to devote a number of hours of time each day to public service broadcasting. Usually this broadcasting is put on when audiences are the smallest. Check up on your local station's public service broadcasting and write an account of what you discover. Is the station genuinely devoted to "public service"?

Further Points of Departure

1. Write an essay with your camera: do a portrait of your family life, a study of your neighborhood, a profile of your town. Take a series of pictures that seem to you to characterize in a coherent way some area of experience with which you are

familiar. Arrange the pictures in an intelligible sequence, and use a minimum of written language to lead the reader through with the effect you want to achieve.

2. Write the essay in 1 in words rather than pictures, and make a comparison of effects. Explore the differences, with particular attention to the possibilities in one medium not present in the other.

3. If you have a movie camera available, try shooting a film that makes some kind of statement about the world, about life, or about experience. Careful planning ahead will help save wasted film and money. A day in the life of a student? A day in the life of a mother at home, involved in the routine of housekeeping? Kids playing games in the neighborhood (fun, arguments, fatigue)? Extremes of wealth and poverty in the city? Advertising as it mars and shapes the local scene? Think up your own subject, and start the shooting. You might want to work up a narrative to accompany the film or you might want to use the reading of a poem, or a recorded piece of music.

4. Select a poem that you like and attempt to capture its mood in a sequence of slides or in a motion picture. You might begin with a simple poem and capture its meaning visually in abstract forms; or you might begin with an abstract or highly suggestive poem and give it meaning through concrete, identifiable images.

4. Causes and Commitments

Wilhelm Stekel: "The mark of the immature man is that he wants to die nobly for a cause, while the mark of the mature man is that he wants to live humbly for one."
As quoted by J. D. Salinger, *Catcher in the Rye*, 1951.

Within two decades, 1940–1960, events occurred that have irrevocably altered man's relationships to other men and to the natural world. The invention of the computer, the successful splitting of the atom and the invention of fission and fusion bombs, the discovery of the biochemistry of the living cell, the exploration of the planet's surface, the extreme acceleration of population growth and the recognition of the certainty of catastrophe if it continues, the breakdown in the organization of cities, the destruction of the natural environment, the linking up of all parts of the world by means of jet flights and television, the preparations for the building of satellites and the first steps into space, the newly realized possibilities of unlimited energy and synthetic raw materials and, in the more advanced countries, the transformation of man's age-old problems of production into problems of distribution and consumption—all these have brought about a drastic, irreversible division between the generations.

. . . the freeing of men's imagination from the past depends . . . on the development of a new kind of communication with those who are most deeply involved with the future—the young who were born in the new world.

Margaret Mead, *Culture and Commitment: A Study of the Generation Gap,* 1970.

The world exists, there can be no doubt (though some philosophers have called its existence into question). And there exist within men's minds many versions of the world, versions bearing resemblance—some more, some less—to the world as it really is. The infinite multiplicity, the perpetual flow of disparate and random happenings, the rushing stream of objects and structures and people and organizations—all constitute a kind of totality of chaos, obscurely and fragmentarily patterned, that cannot be comprehended as it actually is. As compensation for this inability to comprehend, men make up versions of the world and begin to believe in them as the world. Because the mind cannot take the whole in and form it into an image, it fastens on a part or on a single sequence; and as the imagination casts this version into language, the process of reduction and simplification is intensified, for language in its rage for order designates the single element to symbolize the many and arbitrarily turns multiplicity and diversity into unity and identity.

Bewildered by the incomprehensibility and impenetrability of the world as it really is, men have always sought the single key to understanding it and themselves. The secret of man is, some have said, that he is essentially religious, and the world exists to reveal God to him. Others have said that the secret of man is that he is economic, and is driven to accumulate food, clothing, shelter, and other goods—the world existing to supply all these materials for him. Still others have said that the secret of man is that he is sexual, that he belongs to the world as much as its other creatures, and that, wandering too far from his real nature, he is thus in conflict with a world waiting to accept him in his true physical nature. And there are those who contend that man is essentially intellectual, distinguished by his mind from all other animals, and that the world exists in some way as food for thought—to be brought under man's control through exercise of intellect. There are some who believe that man is simply a bundle of behavioristic reactions to his environment and his fellowmen, that he is really no different in his basic ingredients (though perhaps a little more complex) from the other animals—whose study will (they think) reveal much of man's nature.

Man in all these instances is indulging the freedom of thought granted him by the gift of language. Many more instances could be cited, and many of these cited could be elaborated in more complex and subtle terms. But the point to make here is that men feel the compulsion to create a version of the world, a version of reality, around which or in relation to which they can organize their lives, feelings, thoughts. It is probable that all men live by or in concert with some version of the world, even when they have not consciously described or delineated it for themselves: they take over without questioning some version that their group or subculture or locality communally designed; or they put together, largely unaware, fragments from a variety of sources and piece out the whole by invention and ingenuity. And it is probable that many men live schizophrenic lives, in accord with two or more contradictory versions of the world, without letting one interfere with the other—holding the versions separate in the mind for separate occasions. But to live with no version of the world at all seems to be a contradiction in terms, for no one can long live with chaos, anarchy, or random and meaningless experience.

"You're afraid to live, Paul. That's what's the matter with you. You know about Thoreau and Emerson?"

"A little. About as much as you did before Lasher primed you, I'll bet."

"Anyway, Thoreau was in jail because he wouldn't pay a tax to support the Mexican War. He didn't believe in the war. And Emerson came to jail to see him. 'Henry,' he said, 'why are you here?' And Thoreau said, 'Ralph, why aren't you here?' "

"I should want to go to jail?" said Paul, trying to get some sort of message for himself out of the anecdote.

"You shouldn't let fear of jail keep you from doing what you believe in."

"Well, it doesn't." Paul reflected that the big trouble, really, was finding something to believe in.

Kurt Vonnegut, Jr., *Player Piano*, 1952.

Thus we all create our versions of the world and live out our lives in relation to them. We become involved in causes and commitments as they harmonize or conflict with these versions. And we come together in groups and associations to promote a cause, or to fight one: we sit down and talk, we stand up and argue, we harangue a crowd, we hurtle epithets at each other in defense of our causes. Some people proclaim a cause not because of the cause itself but because of the value of associating with those in service of the cause. Others are so obsessed with the cause that they cannot subordinate themselves to any group in which there might be some slight heresy from the cause. People may be grouped in interesting and illuminating ways other than by the causes they espouse: especially, by the nature of their espousal. There are, for instance, the rigid, the flexible, and the limp. The rigid believers are so obsessed with their version of the world that they can tolerate no doubt of their truth, and are willing to use any and every means to achieve the universal establishment of their version as official and enforced dogma. The flexible believers are willing to entertain challenge, to examine other versions created by other minds, to admit self-doubt as well as general doubt, to change when convinced that they are wrong in part or in whole. The limp believers have no convictions and little basis for forming them, and are willing to shift allegiance not on the basis of issues but on the basis of personal loyalties or whimsical likes and dislikes. Such are the kinds of believers in causes—these and many more kinds in between.

It is possible that in passing from youth to age, we begin as limp or casual believers, become flexible, and finally settle into rigidity of belief. But in any event, few would argue with the assertion that open-minded discussion is better than closed-minded or soft-minded, that flexibility is superior to rigidity and limpidity. Exchange, discussion, or language encounter and confrontation—these are the means for sharpening, refining, or changing beliefs. Since the time in prehistory when man acquired language, it has been generally conceded that these means are superior to the club or the axe. Today there is wide consensus that bombast is preferred to bombing, that debate is better than demolition. But in spite of the consensus, violence continues as part of everyday life—both in "peacetime" cities and in war-torn lands.

Beliefs, causes, and commitments have deep roots within, deeper probably than we often know. We may have aligned our beliefs with our version of the world, which, as we always know so well, we have worked out with meticulous reason and impeccable logic, to fit the facts of the world as it really, in all honesty, is. But in a confrontation concerning our belief, we might be disturbed by the charge of "self-interest," and we might well hear an exposé of how our belief relates to some selfish interest or involvement. We might even be surprised at ourselves when we discover that, indeed, there was a deep connection between belief and self that we had not really thought about before. We might have an elaborate theory as to how lower taxes on the rich would benefit society (but we, it turns out, are rich and would personally benefit). Or we have an ingenious argument that shows the advantages to the community of imposing rent controls (but we, of course do not own housing units; we rent them). It is astonishing how frequently beliefs and philosophical commitments turn out to be grounded in plain economic or other self-interest.

But the truth seems to be that reason and logic have very little to do with the acquisition of deep convictions. We feel, and therefore we believe. We sense the area of our own well-being, and therefore we spin out a philosophy that supports it. This is such a widespread human trait, perhaps even universal, that there is no reason to condemn it. But there is reason to condemn ignorance of it. And there is reason to condemn persistence in a belief that serves only the self, and does positive harm to others and to the group.

I am of the opinion that the definitions of maturity which assail us in such profusion currently are uniformly founded on the tacit hypothesis that human development is linked to human passivity. All that I have encountered assume that adjustment and conformity are the desirable modes of life, and that the closer one comes to a condition of domestication, the more mature one is. None of them, to my knowledge, takes account of man's nature and spirit, of his innate rebelliousness, of his intrinsic values, or of his individuality. With monotonous regularity, these definitions predicate themselves upon, and defend, a society that is everyday and everywhere becoming more and more oppressive. Hence, the standards for mature behavior they advise are those standards that may apply to mature cattle or mature puppets—but not to mature men.

Norman Mailer, *Advertisements for Myself,* 1959.

Causes and commitments are, ultimately, ways of structuring and giving meaning to our lives. In our version of the world, perhaps, poverty has no legitimate place. We may then devote ourselves to the elimination of poverty. What does it matter whether we concluded against poverty not because of statistical proofs or ingenious argument, but because of a ride through a slum where we saw dirty, crowded, garbage-strewn streets and felt a strong sympathy for the suffering people? The emotional response to the experience was more convincing than a thousand arguments. But it must be admitted that feelings are treacherous, and can betray us, or simply fulfill our wishes. Perhaps our antagonist on a poverty program also rode through the slum, and saw there sloth, waste, and sheer laziness in the people aimlessly milling about. His quite different emotional response brought him to quite different convictions. In the confrontation of the two sets of convictions, only open minds can assure a dialogue that will go someplace different from where it has already been.

4. CAUSES AND COMMITMENTS   177

People try to put us down
Just because we get around.
Things they do look awful cold
Hope I die before I get old.

This is my generation, baby.

Why don't you all f-f-f-fade away
Don't try and dig what we all say
I'm not trying to cause a big sensation
I'm just talking 'bout my generation.

This is my generation, baby,
My generation.

> Peter Townshend,
> "My Generation," 1965.

There is almost universal agreement in the current age that there is a "generation gap," a gap between the versions of the world created by the older generation and the versions created by the young. Margaret Mead, in *Culture and Commitment: A Study of the Generation Gap* (1970), has contended that the events of 1940–60 (see the epigraph by her, this section) so radically changed the world that those who grew to maturity before this period, the older generation, cannot "know" what the new generation "knows" from the experience of growing up with all the radical changes. Clearly what the younger generation "knows" is not so much a body of knowledge as a set of feelings and attitudes shaped by the events of 1940–60; the feelings and attitudes of the older generation, on the other hand, were shaped by earlier periods—World War I, or the roaring Twenties, or the depressed Thirties. However powerful the impact of the events of those times, it cannot be compared in intensity and shock to the impact of the events since 1940. Both the older and the younger generations "know" these later events that have revolutionized and permanently altered the world, but only the younger generation knows them as deeply shaping experiences: the imagination of the older generation remains fixed on the past, on the Depression or earlier; the younger generation has developed imaginations fixed on a future marked by disaster and holocaust—that future, incidentally, which is primarily theirs, their "inheritance" from the older generation.

The world-versions held by the two generations have not been constructed by reason and logic, then, but are rooted in imaginations shaped by different experiences, one fixed on the past, the other on the future. Clusters of causes and commitments spring out from these bases, and issues and generations are joined in conflict and combat. Margaret Mead has asserted that a new period has arrived in the history of man when adults must "learn" from their children, when the older must "learn" from the younger generation. What must be learned is obviously not technical or technological knowledge (adults have more of this than they need already), but imaginative and experiential "knowledge," a "knowledge" about the future that belongs to them. Margaret Mead calls for a "new kind of communication" between the generations. Whatever elements the new communication might have, we can be certain that the frame will be language, and the substance largely the imagination— or the imaginative grasp of bewildering events and chaotic and swiftly speeding experience. This new communication, if it comes, will bring about a desperately needed reconciliation of the imaginations of both old and young, thereby creating once again new versions of the world— versions which begin with the present and include once again both past and future.

4. CAUSES AND COMMITMENTS   179

Rosewater said an interesting thing to Billy one time about a book that wasn't science fiction. He said that everything there was to know about life was in The Brothers Karamazov, by Feodor Dostoevsky. "But that isn't enough any more," said Rosewater.

Kurt Vonnegut, Jr., *Slaughterhouse Five
or The Children's Crusade,* 1969.

Ideas and Experiments

1. Using the Stekel quotation (in the epigraph) as a starting point, explore the differences between an immature and a mature man.

2. In Margaret Mead's quotation (in the epigraph), she suggests that the differences between the generations have come about for historical reasons—some of which she lists. Explore the ways in which the world has been changed by the events she records, and discuss the reasons these events have produced a radically different individual.

3. Do a character study of someone you know who is
    a. a rigid believer,
    b. a flexible believer, or
    c. a limp believer.

4. Examine your own personality and show how you would classify yourself as to strength of convictions. Have you ever pretended to have strong convictions when you didn't have? Write an account of the experience and why it came about.

5. Explore the self-interest that appears to be at the base of someone's belief. Examine the arguments he has used in defending his beliefs.

6. Trace one of your strong convictions either to self-interest or to an emotional experience that you had. If you can find neither, determine if you can the source of your conviction and write a historical account of its development.

Further Points of Departure

1. Assume, as Margaret Mead does, that the older generation has an imagination fixed on the past, while the younger generation has an imagination fixed on the future. What would you suggest for the "new kind of communication" that she says is needed? What are the ingredients necessary? What are the conditions that might be created to bring about this new communication? What are some of the things that might be discussed between the generations? How might the two imaginations be reconciled?

2. Theodore Roszak, in *The Making of a Counter Culture* (1969), says in his opening paragraph:

The struggle of the generations is one of the obvious constants of human affairs. One stands in peril of some presumption, therefore, to suggest that the rivalry between young and adult in Western society during the current decade is uniquely critical. And yet it is necessary to risk such presumption if one is not to lose sight of our most important contemporary source of radical dissent and cultural innovation. For better or worse, most of what is presently happening that is new, provocative, and engaging in politics, education, the arts, social relations (love, courtship, family, community), is the creation either of youth who are profoundly, even fanatically, alienated from the parental generation, or of those who address themselves primarily to the young. It is at the level of youth that significant social criticism now looks for a responsive hearing as, more and more, it grows to be the common expectation that the young should be those who act, who make things happen, who take the risks, who generally provide the ginger. It would be of interest in its own right that the age-old process of generational disaffiliation should now be transformed from a peripheral experience in the life of the individual and the family into a major lever of radical social change. But if one believes, as I do, that the alienated young are giving shape to something that looks like the saving vision our endangered civilization requires, then there is no avoiding the need to understand and to educate them in what they are about.[7]

a. Agree or disagree, substantiate or qualify, in a response to this point of view. Speak out of your own firsthand, personal experience of being and living the life of a youth who has known adults intimately and long.

b. Explore the whole of Roszak's book and evaluate how well he backs up his belief. Another book on the subject that you might want to take a look at: Charles Reich, *The Greening of America* (1970).

7. Theodore Roszak, *The Making of a Counter Culture* (Garden City, N.Y.: Anchor Books–Doubleday & Co., 1969), p. 1.

VI. THE INDIVIDUAL VOICE: STYLES PRIVATE AND PUBLIC

1. Personal Writing

. . . the essence of a sound style is that it cannot be reduced to rules —that it is a living and breathing thing, with something of the demoniacal in it—that it fits its proprietor tightly and yet ever so loosely, as his skin fits him. It is, in fact, quite as securely an integral part of him as that skin is. It hardens as his arteries harden. It is gaudy when he is young and gathers decorum when he grows old. On the day after he makes a mash on a new girl it glows and glitters. If he has fed well, it is mellow. If he has gastritis it is bitter. In brief, a style is always the outward and visible symbol of a man, and it cannot be anything else. To attempt to teach it is as silly as to set up courses in making love.

H. L. Mencken, *A Mencken Chrestomathy*, 1926.

The problem of doing justice to the implicit, the imponderable, and the unknown is of course not unique to politics. It is always with us in science, it is with us in the most trivial of personal affairs, and it is one of the great problems of writing and of all forms of art. It is style which complements affirmation with limitation and with humility; it is style which makes it possible to act effectively, but not absolutely; it is style which, in the domain of foreign policy, enables us to find a harmony between the pursuit of ends essential to us and the regard for the views, the sensibilities, the aspirations of those to whom the problem may appear in another light; it is style which is the deference that action pays to uncertainty; it is above all style through which power defers to reason.

J. Robert Oppenheimer, *The Open Mind*, 1955.

In many ways it is best to think of all writing as personal writing. Someone, once puzzled by the term "personal experience," remarked: "I've never had an experience that wasn't personal." Some such view may well be applied to writing. What is "personal writing"? It is hard to conceive of writing worthy of attention that is not in some sense personal. Writing requires that a single individual, summoning all the strength of his individuality, retire to solitude (in spirit, if not in fact), and there speak with his own voice on paper. He may speak on any subject; he may choose any method or form; and he may fulfill any purpose he chooses. The one constant that runs through all the subjects possible and all the forms invented, and all the purposes chosen is—the writer's voice, his distinctive accent as it is transferred from interior depths to the blank sheet of paper. The voice may be so much his own that the writer cannot even hear it himself. Or he may have been badly (and sadly) trained to try always to suppress the personal sound in his writing. But unless he has turned himself into a machine or computer, his voice will out. And a good thing, too.

So many people have been indoctrinated with the view that good writing is primarily "correct" writing, and that the best writing is "objective" and "impersonal" (and therefore devoid of the first-person singular), that there is abroad in the country an "ideal" prose that is so correct, objective, and impersonal that it is almost unreadable. This prose pours out of government offices, universities, businesses; has become a kind of establishment prose; and might be described as the prose in the gray flannel suit. It is a faceless and voiceless prose: the sound that arises from it is monotonous and boring. In many cases the attempt is made to make it appear, rather than the sound of a human voice, the proclamation of an establishment, the oracular declaration of an organization. The following passage, for example, has been taken from a government document explaining the operation of a series of clearinghouses established to handle the great flood of scholarship on education:

The nearly explosive expansion of education resources has triggered an equivalent proliferation of written material. A significant proportion of what is currently appropriate and of merit too often is not reported in sources readily available to the greatest number of potential users. There is a need for a comprehensive and structured means of information exchange. Methods must be found for organizing and distilling this information in order more effectively to channel the efforts of researchers and practitioners toward the utilization of all available data and resources. Experience suggests that there would be unnecessary duplication and wasted effort if information handling agencies or clearinghouses were to develop autonomously. The problem, consequently, reduces to one of establishing a network of specialized clearinghouses designed to meet the need for information retrieval in education while avoiding the hazards of independent development. To this end the Educational Research Information Center of the United States Office of Education is developing a network of information centers in the field of education so that information may be most efficiently acquired, stored, retrieved and exchanged among the cooperating units and other members of the educational community.[1]

Few people will be lured into reading beyond the first line of this passage. It is marked not only by monotony but also by pomposity. It seems swollen with its own importance. It achieves a kind of pseudo-objectivity in its severe suppression of all personal reference, in its pretentious vocabulary, in its elaborate statement of the obvious. It seems swollen monstrously with its own importance; and we have the feeling that if we could stick a pin in

1. A fugitive publication issued by the Department of Health, Education and Welfare, Office of Education.

some vital spot, the air would rush out, and the entire passage would sag and collapse on the floor in a pitiful little puddle.

What is the sound of the personal voice in writing? It is harder to define it than it is to simply show it. Henry David Thoreau's voice sounds loud and clear in his work, and the tone can be caught in a single sentence, as in this one from *Walden:* "I would rather sit on a pumpkin and have it all to myself than be crowded on a velvet cushion."[2]

But the sound of the human voice also comes through in this paragraph by an eleven-year-old Harlem resident:

My block is the most terrible block I've ever seen. There are at lease 25 or 30 narcartic people in my block. The cops come around there and tries to act bad but I bet inside of them they are as scared as can be. They even had in the papers that this block is the worst block, not in Manhattan but in New York City. In the summer, they don't do nothing except shooting, shaving, and fighting. They hang all over the stoops and when you say excuse me to them they hear you but they just don't feel like moving. Some times they make me so mad that I feel like slaping them and stuffing an bag of garbage down their throats. Theres only one policeman who can handle these people and we all call him "sunny." When he come around in his cop car the people run around the corners, and he wont let anyone sit on the stoops. If you don't believe this story come around some time and you'll find out.[3]

And here is the sound of the human voice in a passage from LeRoi Jones:

2. Henry David Thoreau, *Walden and Civil Disobedience,* ed. Owen Thomas (New York: W. W. Norton & Co., 1966), p. 25.
3. Herbert R. Kohl, *Teaching the "Unteachable"* (New York: *The New York Review of Books,* 1967), p. 15.

VI. THE INDIVIDUAL VOICE

For those of you who do not know my name, I am what is called "A Negro Writer." I write what is commonly called "Negro Literature." What these terms usually mean (I mean somewhere below the veil of anxious politeness smart Americans think of as their image) is that the people who can be tagged with them produce a variety of writing that should be thought of as second rate, in much the same way all American literature was thought of before Melville, Poe, James, etc. But the reasons for this low estimate of black writing have not, I think, been fully understood. And I mean the estimate made by the official estimators, the deciders of what is of intellectual, hence emotional, value in the society, *i.e.*, what can be carried off and deposited in that huge junk heap of useless artifacts called Culture.[4]

And, finally, here is the personal voice of Norman Mailer at the opening of his book of essays, *Advertisements for Myself:*

Like many another vain, empty, and bullying body of our time, I have been running for President these last ten years in the privacy of my mind, and it occurs to me that I am less close now than when I began. Defeat has left my nature divided, my sense of timing is eccentric, and I contain within myself the bitter exhaustions of an old man, and the cocky arguments of a bright boy. So I am everything but my proper age of thirty-six, and anger has brought me to the edge of the brutal. In sitting down to write a sermon for this collection, I find arrogance in much of my mood.[5]

These randomly selected samples of prose should suffice to demonstrate the actual presence of the voice in writing. But just

4. LeRoi Jones, "LeRoi Jones Talking," *Home: Social Essays* (New York: William Morrow & Co., 1966) pp. 180–81.
5. Norman Mailer, *Advertisements for Myself* (New York: G. P. Putnam's Sons, 1959; reprinted New York: Signet Books–New American Library, 1960), p. 15.

as it would be difficult to point to the actual sound in a particular cluster of words, so it would be difficult to separate the sound from the tone of frankness, candor, and simple honesty that comes through these passages. They are all marked by the unobtrusive presence of the first-person singular.

Whatever the voice is and however it is manifested in the written word, it in effect *is* the style. Writing is an expression of personality, and the personality makes itself manifest in the style, or voice. Style, then, is not something—a technique—that can be learned, anymore than one can "learn" his personality. But the writer can do something about his style. He can first discard the inhibitions that have been acquired over a long period, and from the authority frequently of the schools and of the society: the inhibitions that keep the "I" off the page, that suppress the individuality of view and experience, and that encourage the impersonal at the expense of the personal. And he can next strive for that frankness and candor that mark the passages quoted above: this means that he would avoid fulfilling expectations with the clichés that are expected, and instead discover within himself his genuine feelings, point of view, and perspective—and express them.

. . . I don't think that style is consciously arrived at, any more than one arrives at the color of one's eyes. After all, your style is you. At the end the personality of a writer has so much to do with the work. The personality has to be humanly there. Personality is a debased word, I know, but it's what I mean. The writer's individual humanity, his word or gesture toward the world, has to appear almost like a character that makes contact with the reader.

Truman Capote, *Writers at Work: The Paris Review Interviews*, 1958.

VI. THE INDIVIDUAL VOICE

Just as style ultimately is the honest expression of the individual self, so it is inseparable from substance and meaning. It is sometimes assumed that the essence of writing is the "content," and that the content is bodied forth in one of any possible number of styles. In this view, the writer has his idea and then chooses the style in which to clothe it. But words are simply not that specific and stable and precise in their meanings. To change the words is to change the meaning. To change the style of any piece of writing is to change the substance, content, and impact of the writing. In the deepest and most subtle sense, the style *is* the meaning of any verbal expression. And as the style is an extension of the self, it is well to be aware of one's own style—just as it is well to be aware of one's individuality. But to effect change in the style means to effect—alas—change in the self (or to release or deepen or discover it).

A note of warning should be added. Liberal use of the first-person singular does not convert a drab style into a lively one. There are, obviously, times when there is no need to use "I," when, in fact, it would be obtrusive and even pretentious. And it should be stressed that there can be a distinctive voice in a passage of prose without the appearance of "I" (see the H. L. Mencken epigraph to this section). The worst kind of voice to encounter in writing is that of self-conscious cuteness and a forced journalistic breeziness. Cuteness is no more attractive in a style than in a personality. What we appreciate in both is the relaxed, unpretentious, natural self.

Ideas and Suggestions

1. Compare the definitions of style of Mencken and Oppenheimer. Are they in conflict, or is there a way of reconciling them?

2. Reflect on an incident of which you have personal knowledge. Discuss the difficulties of composing an impersonal or objective account of the incident, and speculate as to some of the

various accounts that might be given from various points of view.

3. Find a piece of homogenized or computerized prose and analyze its meaning and its effect.

4. Probe the nature of your own voice in writing by looking over a series of pieces that you have written in the past. Can you define the character of your voice?

5. Attempt to isolate an idea apart from its language, and then embody the idea in a number of ways. Does the idea remain constant, or does the language changing subtly change the idea? Discuss.

6. Rewrite the passage on educational clearinghouses in what you would consider readable prose. Try one version in which the essential meaning is retained but the air is let out of the prose. Try another version that somehow includes your voice.

Further Points of Departure

If you have been trying for a long time to extinguish the personal self in your writing, it might be difficult to find your voice. Try a series of experiments in which you let yourself go.

1. Write a description of some event that struck you as more important than generally believed, or of some event that seemed to you as less important than assumed—preferably an event in which you were involved as a participant or witness. Emphasize your perspective, the way it struck you, or bored you, or seemed trivial in spite of its magnification (or overwhelming in spite of its trivialization by others).

2. Write a personal account, in the idiom you would use in talking with a close friend, of one of the following experiences (maybe you have just called him on the phone):

> an exam that you flubbed because . . .
> a date that turned out to be dull because . . .
> a surprise gift for a special friend

3. Begin an essay with the most outrageous opinion you can invent that is not so far from the truth as to be unbelievable. Then show how you sometimes believe part of what you have just expressed. You will have to tease the reader a little along the way.

4. Complete the following essay: "Most of my friends are convinced that I am meek, wishy-washy, passive, and timid. As a matter of fact, I have fooled them all." Of course, your opener should be your own invention in your own voice. How do your friends look at you? Are you really like that? What deceptions have you practiced on them? What do you sometimes act out in your fantasy life?

5. If you had ten minutes with the President (of the company, college, or country), what would you tell him in your own voice and with your own words?

2. *Variations and Varieties of Voice*

There are many reasons why we forget things that we have noticed or experienced; and there are just as many ways in which they may be recalled to mind. An interesting example is that of cryptomnesia, or "concealed recollection." An author may be writing steadily to a preconceived plan, working out an argument or developing the line of a story, when he suddenly runs off at a tangent. Perhaps a fresh idea has occurred to him, or a different image, or a whole new sub-plot. If you ask him what prompted the digression, he will not be able to tell you. He may not even have noticed the change, though he has now produced material that is entirely fresh and apparently unknown to him before. Yet it can sometimes be shown convincingly that what he has written bears a striking similarity to the work of another author—a work that he believes he has never seen.

Carl G. Jung, "Approaching the Unconscious,"
Man and His Symbols, 1964 (post.).

Questions about style can most usefully be approached if we think of a style as the expression of a personality. I do not mean at all that our words necessarily reveal what we are "really like." I do mean that every writer and talker, more or less consciously, chooses a role which he thinks appropriate to express for a given time and situation. The personality I am expressing in this written sentence is not the same as the one I orally express to my three-year-old who at this moment is bent on climbing onto my typewriter. For each of these two situations, I choose a different "voice," a different mask, in order to accomplish what I want accomplished.

Walker Gibson, *The Limits of Language*, 1962.

Few people have been willing to admit that writing has its mysteries. The most marked of these is the simple mystery of the flow of words from the self to the page—the flow that rushes at times, slows at other times to a sluggish pace, and sometimes dries to a mere trickle or to absolutely nothing at all. There are times when the flow can be channeled in a definite direction, when there is supremely conscious control of everything the stream of words carries; but at other times the flow is stubbornly self-guided, refusing any orders from the conscious mind and turning off into directions that we had not wanted or anticipated. Sometimes we are pleased at writing what we set out to write, but at other times we are surprised at writing something that we did not intend and perhaps don't even fully understand.

The emotions of writing—or of attempting to write—are surprisingly varied and deeply felt. There is, indeed, something quite intimidating about an empty page ready to be used, but still in possession of its pure virgin whiteness. Even when we are filled with some subject or idea or some emotion that we want desperately to express, it often takes a major act of will to begin making the black marks on the white paper. If the flow of words runs smoothly, and we like what we say after we say it, we may have that feeling of elation that is peculiar to writing well—a sense of self-fulfillment in creation. And as the feeling gives us satisfaction and confidence, the flow increases, and writing begins to seem effortless—although the concentration will take its toll in psychic energy.

> One takes a piece of paper, anything, the flat of a shingle, slate, cardboard and with anything handy to the purpose begins to put down the words after the desired expression in mind. This is the anarchical phase of writing. The blankness of the writing surface may cause the mind to shy, it may be impossible to release the faculties. Write, write anything: it is all in all probability worthless anyhow, it is never hard to destroy written characters. But it is absolutely essential to the writing of anything worthwhile that the mind be fluid and release itself to the task.
>
> William Carlos Williams, "How to Write," 1936.

But frequently the flow will not start. The page remains stubbornly white. Anger and frustration set in, and we begin to long to be someplace else, anyplace else, rather than in front of a desk chewing a pencil over a blank page. We run to get a drink of water. We go sharpen a pencil. We arrange the paperclips in fancy bracelets and necklaces. We decide that we must reread our notes, or look over again the article that seemed so good—or bad —on our subject. And we may finally get up and leave the white sheet of paper triumphantly white on the desk, as we take a walk or throw a basketball or go to a movie.

Sometimes it is possible to trick the flow into starting. It might be such a simple thing as beginning defiantly to write on the white page whatever comes into the mind—something like a warming-up exercise to set the creative juices trickling through the mental channels. It might be making a list of random thoughts that can be sorted through later, put in order, discarded, or revised. It might be such a ridiculous thing as standing on one's head or walking rapidly in circles. There is no reason not to try some of these tricks, and it is possible that you might discover some of your own that no one else has thought of.

For it is true that there is a part of the self that seems sometimes recalcitrant and self-willed. It must be coaxed or tricked into doing our bidding. And in the actual writing process, there is also sometimes a self that insists on getting on paper without our knowledge or intent. Carl Jung describes this phenomenon (see epigraph): a writer is following a plan, and moving ahead within it, but suddenly goes off unintentionally on a tangent. The writer thinks in one direction, but the pencil moves in another: it seems almost to develop a life and will of its own. And the writer looks with amazement on what he finally writes. He might even discover that this tangent runs contrary to the main current of what he is attempting to write. Indeed, it is not at all uncommon for a writer to begin writing in one direction, and conclude pointed in another—all to his own surprise. The human mind works in mysterious ways, and it is often difficult to figure out just what it is up to. But it seems understandable that a writer who starts to write from one point of view may discover in the constant stream of thinking and rethinking involved in writing that he has roiled the waters sufficiently to cause another point of view, perhaps more attractive or more persuasive, to surface and assert its presence. As this point of view makes its way to the page, the total piece of writing gradually becomes schizophrenic. There obviously arises the necessity for revision, after some searching self-questioning and self-reviewing.

In situations of this kind, where and what is the role of the self in the process of writing? It is, clearly, no easy task to follow the injunction to let the self go on paper. What self? Which self? How many selves? There are, perhaps surprisingly, some choices to be made. There are some choices, but not an infinite number. We all know that there is a limit to the range of selves that we can decide to be. And we all know, too, that the classic writers have generally embodied themselves in their work in one dominant identity. A glance at two passages from Emily Dickinson and Walt Whitman can leave no doubt as to which lines belong to which poet:

> I'm Nobody! Who are you?
> Are you—Nobody—Too?
> Then there's a pair of us!
> Don't tell! they'd banish us—you know!
>
> How dreary—to be—Somebody!
> How public—like a Frog—
> To tell your name—the livelong June—
> To an admiring Bog![6]

❊   ❊   ❊   ❊   ❊

Walt Whitman, a kosmos, of Manhattan the son,
Turbulent, fleshy, sensual, eating, drinking and breeding,
No sentimentalist, no stander above men and women or apart
   from them,
No more modest than immodest.

Unscrew the locks from the doors!
Unscrew the doors themselves from their jambs!

Whoever degrades another degrades me,
And whatever is done or said returns at last to me.

6. Emily Dickinson, *The Complete Poems of Emily Dickinson,* ed. Thomas H. Johnson (Boston: Little, Brown, 1960), p. 133.

2. VARIATIONS AND VARIETIES OF VOICE   195

Through me the afflatus surging and surging, through me the
current and index.[7]

Even without Whitman's name in his poem, and even without
wide acquaintance with their poetry, it is no difficult task to
assign the right lines to Whitman and the right ones (the first
set) to Emily Dickinson. It seems absurd to us now that one
critic, back in the nineteenth century, advised Emily Dickinson
to become the female Walt Whitman of America. She was clearly
incapable of assuming the kind of expansive and aggressive identity that marked Whitman's every line. And he was certainly
incapable of writing in her shy, delicate, hushed voice.

But though Emily Dickinson cannot be Whitman, nor Whitman, Dickinson, it is still true that we have some choice in the
selection of self in writing, some choice in the tone and color of
voice with which we speak. Just as we assume many roles in our
lives, one in our family, another in the classroom, still another in
a dormitory, and another on the job, and many more—so we are
able to speak in many different voices, ranging through several
degrees of informality all the way up to the strictest formality.
If we gossip with a friend, we speak in a tone of voice that would
be inappropriate for delivering a eulogy at a funeral. And the
tone at the funeral would be incongruous in a classroom discussion, and the tone for the classroom would be jarring if used in a
formal speech at a formal dinner.

So too in writing, we unconsciously or consciously adjust our
voice to fit our audience. We assume a role that is appropriate for
the occasion and the readers, and we speak on the page with the
voice of that self. This does not mean that we are being insincere
or hypocritical, any more than we are betraying a "true self" when
we play many roles throughout the day or throughout our life.
The true self contains and embraces all these roles, and there will

7. Walt Whitman, *Complete Poetry and Selected Prose,* ed. James E.
Miller, Jr. (Boston: Houghton Mifflin Co., 1959), p. 41.

VI. THE INDIVIDUAL VOICE

be common elements to all of them that will still make an identifiable identity, a distinctive individuality, in spite of the several selves that we play.

There is another important sense in which the nature of the audience will affect the way we say what we say. If the audience is going to *read* our words, we will put them together in a way somewhat different from the way intended for an audience assembled to *hear* our words read aloud. We all realize that when we write, we use language somewhat differently from the way we use it when conversing with friends or acquaintances. In writing, we cut repetitions; we straighten out tangled expressions; we complete sentences often left dangling in mid air; we find words to substitute for the "body language" of a pointed finger or a lifted eyebrow. Just as we go through a process of editing in moving from casual talk to writing, so we modify the nature of our writing in accordance with whether it is being prepared for the eye or the ear, to be read or to be heard.

What these modifications must be is difficult to say. But we have all had the experience of finding a paragraph of prose incomprehensible when read aloud by its author, but understandable when read (and perhaps reread) in silence by us. Obviously, prose written for silent, contemplative reading can be more dense, more elliptical, more complex because the reader has time to slow down, to reread, to savor subtleties that would be lost on the ear. Moreover, prose written to be read aloud to an audience, in the form of a speech, needs to be informed with the sense of an event, an occasion, with its own psychological structure. Such prose must not only be lucid on a single *hearing*, but must be paced in such a way—alternating moments of relaxation with moments of intensity—as to enable the listeners to follow and retain the main thread of the discussion or discourse. Repetition which might appear awkward in an essay could be a necessity in a speech.

Common sense based on one's own experience as reader and listener will reveal still other differences between prose written to be read and prose written to be heard. One way of testing one's own writing is to read it aloud, to oneself or a friend. Such a reading will frequently reveal weaknesses that remain weaknesses whether the prose is intended for hearing or seeing. It will also pick up sentences and paragraphs that seem harmless to the eye, but whose stumbling and awkward rhythms trip the tongue of the speaker and dissipate all emphasis and point. Thus, reading aloud can prove a valuable exercise in revision in any writing experience; but for writing written to be heard rather than seen, reading aloud is a necessary part of the fundamental process of composition.

The writer, then, needs to glance in several directions as he writes. He must keep an eye both on his audience and on the nature of the occasion for his writing. The tone of his voice must be tuned to that audience and occasion. But at the same time he must keep another eye on that hard core of the self, the only source of his distinction and identity, and attune his voice to its deepest vibrations. And throughout the process he must be alert to the runaway selves that might move out and take over, without so much as asking permission. He must not dismiss these defiant selves too quickly: they might reveal to him much that he simply did not—or refused to—know before they appeared.

Ideas and Experiments

1. Describe as vividly as you can the actual experience of writing one of the papers you have already written.

2. Have you discovered a particularly effective trick for starting the flow of language on the page? Write an account of how you discovered it and how it works.

3. Have you ever been surprised by what you have written? Have you ever changed your mind in the middle of writing an opinion about some matter? Explore the causes for this happening in your own case.

4. Try writing a prose paragraph in the "voice" of Emily Dickinson or Whitman.

5. Attempt to write the same matter in two different styles or voices, for widely separated audiences—one extremely informal, the other formal. Then analyze the inevitable differences, subtle and oblique, in meaning.

Further Points of Departure

When ideas refuse to flow, it is well to remember that language may be the best spur to thought. And it is possible that the best way to let language flood in and move the mind off dead center is to sacrifice the first piece of white paper to doodling and experimenting, writing down whatever comes to mind, and then writing down what that brings to mind, and then jumping over to a completely unrelated notion and jotting that down. "Get black on white," as De Maupassant advised. This exercise not only limbers up the fingers and reduces white-paper panic, but it starts the flow, and if luck holds, turns into a flood that cannot be dammed.

1. Try flipping through the dictionary and letting a chance-encountered word start off a train of associations—hairball, helpmate, levee, marksman, nothing, sigh.

2. Try "automatic" writing, letting the pen move across the page creating sentences that are not calculated ahead of time. Let sentence flow on sentence, no matter how nonsensical.

3. Take some encouragement, inspiration, or amusement from a completely strange and perhaps incomprehensible writer. Here is a paragraph from Gertrude Stein's "Composition as Explanation": "The composition is the thing seen by every one living in the living they are doing, they are the composing of the composition that at the time they are living is the composition of the time in which they are living. It is that that makes living a thing they are doing. Nothing else is different, of that almost any one can be

certain. The time when and the time of and the time in that composition is the natural phenomena of that composition and of that perhaps every one can be certain."[8]

4. Write nonsense that makes a kind of sense; write sense that is really nonsense. In any event, write!

5. If all fails, go to bed. Perhaps you will have a dream or a nightmare that can serve as the inspirational center of your essay.

8. Gertrude Stein, "Composition as Explanation," *Selected Writings of Gertrude Stein* (New York: Modern Library–Random House, 1962), p. 516.

3. *Two Poles of Style*

. . . I always try to write on the principle of the iceberg. There is seven-eighths of it underwater for every part that shows. Anything you know you can eliminate and it only strengthens your iceberg. It is the part that doesn't show. If a writer omits something because he does not know it then there is a hole in the story.

Ernest Hemingway, *Writers at Work: The Paris Review Interviews, Second Series,* 1963.

The germ [of my style—including long "run-on sentences" and "vague pronoun references"] of it was a special purpose—not at all to be obscure. I think that any artist, musician, writer, painter would like to take all of the experience which he has seen, observed, felt and reduce that to one single color or tone or word, which is impossible. In fact, he would like to reduce all human experience onto the head of the pin as the man engraved the Lord's Prayer on the head of a pin once. He can't do that, but he is still going to try. And the obscurity, the prolixity which you find in writers is simply that desire to put all that experience into one word. Then he has got to add another word, another word becomes a sentence, but he's still trying to get it into one unstopping whole—a paragraph or a page—before he finds a place to put a full stop. The style—I think the story the writer is trying to tell invents, compels its style. That no writer has got the time to be obscure for the sake of obscurity. It's because at that moment he couldn't think of any better way to tell the story he was trying to tell.

William Faulkner, *Faulkner at West Point,* 1964.

There is a view of writing prevalent that places emphasis on brevity, simplicity, directness, bluntness, plainness. The advice is sometimes given as though it came from on high that it is better to use short words than long words; that it is better to write a series of short sentences than a long, complicated one; that it is better to go to the heart of the matter than to circle around it; that it is better to be plain than to be complex and risk obscurity; that it is better, above all, to be clear and lucid than to be vague or cloudy (even though the subject itself tends to be illusive and opaque).

It is, of course, difficult to quarrel with all these "rules" for good writing, but at the same time it is impossible to endorse all of them without expressing some reservations. There are instances when all these rules appear to be applicable. But there are also times when they don't seem relevant. There are instances when a job of writing requires long words, complicated sentences, an oblique or circular approach to a fragile center. And there are instances when to be absolutely clear and lucid is to distort and falsify, to give only the appearance of simplicity when, in reality, the subject remains steeped in obscurity and complexity.

There is, in point of fact, no "best style" for all writers. And the prevalent view that everyone should write in the same simplistic style is based on a misunderstanding of the nature of language and the writing process. The best style for any writer will be one that takes into account his own temperament and personality, the requirements of his subject, and the nature of his audience. On some occasions these may call for long words rather than short, for complicated sentences rather than simple, for an intentional opaqueness rather than a distorting lucidity. They might call, indeed, for a torrent of words rather than a trickle, for a flood of rhetoric rather than a rivulet.

The ideal of the simplistic style may be traced to historical sources. There was a time when Ernest Hemingway was the literary idol of the world, and particularly the academic world. Nobody before Hemingway had ever discovered such rich possibilities in the utterly stripped, monosyllabic, bare-bones style. Here is a paragraph from his famous novel, *The Sun Also Rises* (1926):

She turned quickly and went into the hotel. The chauffeur drove me around to my flat. I gave him twenty francs and he touched his cap and said: "Good night, sir," and drove off. I rang the bell. The door opened and I went up-stairs and went to bed.[9]

It must in all fairness be pointed out that this passage comes at the end of a chapter and, in context, captures and evokes a mood that appears absolutely appropriate to the situation in the action of the novel; the stripped-down style underscores the stripped-down spirits of the characters in the novel. In short, the style not only takes meaning from the action and situation but gives meaning to them as well. And this style has all the attributes that are so frequently called for in handbooks on writing.

But as we appeal to literary history we must not forget another

9. Ernest Hemingway, *The Sun Also Rises* (New York: Charles Scribner's Sons, 1926), p. 65.

writer whose reputation was slower to develop than Hemingway's, but who now stands as perhaps the preeminent American writer of the twentieth century: William Faulkner. In style Faulkner is poles apart from Hemingway. Here is his opening paragraph from *Absalom, Absalom!* (1936):

From a little after two oclock until almost sundown of the long still hot weary dead September afternoon they sat in what Miss Coldfield still called the office because her father had called it that—a dim hot airless room with the blinds all closed and fastened for forty-three summers because when she was a girl someone had believed that light and moving air carried heat and that dark was always cooler, and which (as the sun shone fuller and fuller on that side of the house) became latticed with yellow slashes full of dust motes which Quentin thought of as being flecks of the dead old dried paint itself blown inward from the scaling blinds as wind might have blown them. There was a wistaria vine blooming for the second time that summer on a wooden trellis before one window, into which sparrows came now and then in random gusts, making a dry vivid dusty sound before going away; and opposite Quentin, Miss Coldfield in the eternal black which she had worn for forty-three years now, whether for sister, father, or nothusband and none knew, sitting so bolt upright in the straight hard chair that was so tall for her that her legs hung straight and rigid as if she had iron shinbones and ankles, clear of the floor with that air of impotent and static rage like children's feet, and talking in that grim haggard amazed voice until at last listening would renege and hearing-sense self-confound and the long-dead object of her impotent yet indomitable frustration would appear, as though by outraged recapitulation evoked, quiet inattentive and harmless, out of the biding and dreamy and victorious dust.[10]

10. William Faulkner, *Absalom, Absalom!* (New York: Modern Library–Random House, 1936), p. 7.

This passage violates almost all the rules of good writing that are found in almost all the handbooks. There are only two sentences in the paragraph, and the sentences are crammed full of detail, some of it stuffed between sets of parentheses, some of it simply jammed in without benefit of warning from punctuation. Many of the words are multisyllabic—*impotent, indomitable, recapitulation*—and some of them seem to add little in meaning (but much in mood). But however much this passage might seem to violate the rules of good style, the fact is that it is a brilliant beginning of a brilliant novel, one of the great novels of the twentieth century.

It must, of course, be noted that the two passages from Hemingway and Faulkner are from works of fiction. Some would claim that this makes the difference in what is allowable in style. And it must be granted that these passages are stylistically directed to the fictional purposes and directions of the two writers. But when all is said and done, there is not all that difference between fiction and nonfiction prose. Take the prose style, for instance, of John Milton in *Areopagitica,* or of Walt Whitman in *Democratic Vistas* (both nonfiction works): these works approach in style the complexity and difficulty of the style of the Faulkner passage.

The truth is that different styles serve different purposes. To set up the simple style or the complicated style as the ideal style is to falsify the nature of language, and to invite the falsification of reality. It would be as absurd to ask Faulkner to write like Hemingway as it was to ask Emily Dickinson to write like Whitman. Faulkner would have to betray not only his own temperament but also his novelistic subject—and his audience. Nor could Hemingway be expected to betray his craft to write like Faulkner.

In the epigraphs to this part of the book are two passages from Hemingway and Faulkner, introducing two different metaphors in explanation of their styles. Hemingway describes his writing as based on the principle of the iceberg; only one-eighth shows, while the rest remains in the head. Faulkner develops the prin-

VI. THE INDIVIDUAL VOICE

ciple of the head of the pin, on which, he says, he has tried to crowd all human experience (taking the lead from the man who did engrave the Lord's Prayer on the pin-head). We might use these two images, the iceberg and the head of a pin, as symbols of two kinds of writing, or two approaches to embodying reality in words—as applicable to nonfiction as fiction. There is the human impulse to be spare, lean, brief, letting a little do for a lot —after the manner of the iceberg (hiding much beneath the surface). And there is the human impulse to pour it all out, to crowd it all in or on, to tell it all, to keep trying and spinning in the hopes of finally encompassing the totality—after the manner of crowding something on the head of a pin (so that it will hold all human experience). Neither impulse is "wrong" or "right"; both exist. And both have produced some of the most impressive prose in our literature. Among the "iceberg" writers we might place Henry David Thoreau and Mark Twain, and among the "head of the pin" writers we might place Henry James and Thomas Wolfe. But to mention other writers is simply to remind us that there are not only two styles, but many: we might think of two extremes, one of simplicity, the other of complexity, and then note the multitude of possibilities in between.

Beware, then, of simple rules for good writing. There are obviously times when it is best to break a long sentence up into some short ones, or to choose short words in place of long, or to pare away material that confuses or obscures the point being made. But be skeptical of all generalizations which are supposed to have universal application. They are likely to be misleading if not downright false. What must prevail finally in all decisions about words is the writer's temperament, the subject he is dealing with, and the nature of his audience. Taking into account all of these, the writer must feel his way into an appropriate style, through initial writing, and through several rereadings and revisions.

Ideas and Experiments

1. Re-write the passage from Hemingway the way Faulkner might have written it. Discuss the ways you have changed the meaning and effect.

2. Re-write the passage from Faulkner the way Hemingway might have written it.

3. Select a topic of your own choice, or a bit of action for a short story that you might write. Use first the iceberg approach, and then the head-of-a-pin approach, making each as simple and as complex as possible. Finally, use your own approach. Compare and discuss the three versions.

4. Write an account of your own convictions about writing. How would you describe your temperament—as closer to Hemingway's or to Faulkner's? What rules would you make up for yourself? Do you tend to be wordier than you should be, and do you therefore have to pare your writing in revision? Or do you write sparingly initially, and have to fill out in revision? Or do you always get it just right the first time through?

5. Find some extreme examples of the two kinds of writing described here and compare their elements and effect. Do you have any feelings about which of the two styles is best able to get at or apprehend reality?

Further Points of Departure

Style is never neutral. It works against or for the statement or feeling it presumably carries. At its best, it evokes emotions and provokes responses and underscores meaning. At its worst it evokes apathy and undermines meaning.

1. Explore the Hemingway or Faulkner passages quoted in the text and relate in some detail the style to the meaning.

2. Any analysis of either of these passages should ultimately be

based on context, on the relation of the passages to the remainder of the novels. Read either of the novels and speculate on the suitability of the style to the fictional world created.

3. Conduct a similar experiment on a pair of nonfiction prose texts—say, Margaret Mead's *Culture and Commitment: A Study of the Generation Gap* and R. D. Laing's *The Politics of Experience*.

4. In American literature, Ralph Waldo Emerson is known for his epigrammatic style tending toward the abstract, while Henry David Thoreau is known for his pithy style tending toward the concrete. Find two passages that seem typical (perhaps in "Self-Reliance" and "Civil Disobedience") and compare them as to their effect and success.

5. Use either of these sentences to write a contemporary essay on what they suggest: Ralph Waldo Emerson ("Self-Reliance"): "Whoso would be a man, must be a nonconformist!"[11] Henry David Thoreau ("Civil Disobedience"): "Unjust laws exist; shall we be content to obey them, or shall we endeavor to amend them, and obey them until we have succeeded, or shall we transgress them at once?"[12]

11. Ralph Waldo Emerson, "Self Reliance," *Selections from Ralph Waldo Emerson*, ed. Stephen E. Whicher (Boston: Houghton Mifflin Co., 1957). p. 149.
12. Henry David Thoreau, *The Variorum Civil Disobedience*, ed. Walter Harding (New York: Twayne Publishers, 1967), p. 39.

4. Preserving the Human

When Job's life miscarried, he was able, at least in imagination, to confront God and criticize His ways. But the suppression of personality is already so nearly complete in the automated economy that the reputed heads of our great organizations are as incapable of changing its goals as is the lowliest filing clerk. It is the system that gives orders. As for confronting the principals in person, our auto-matic agencies are as obscure and as bafflingly inaccessible as the authorities Kafka pictures in his accurate and prophetic nightmare "The Trial." Humanly speaking, the proper name for automation is self-inflicted impotence.

Lewis Mumford, "Reflections: Science and Technology III,"
The New Yorker, Oct. 24, 1970.

I decline to accept the end of man. It is easy enough to say that man is immortal simply because he will endure; that when the last ding-dong of doom has clanged and faded from the last worthless rock hanging tideless in the last red and dying evening, that even then there will still be one more sound: that of his puny inexhaustible voice, still talking. I refuse to accept this. I believe that man will not merely endure: he will prevail. He is immortal, not because he alone among creatures has an inexhaustible voice, but because he has a soul, a spirit capable of compassion and sacrifice and endur-ance. The poet's, the writer's, duty is to write about these things. It is his privilege to help man endure by lifting his heart, by remind-ing him of the courage and honor and hope and pride and com-passion and pity and sacrifice which have been the glory of his past. The poet's voice need not merely be the record of man, it can be one of the props, the pillars to help him endure and prevail.

William Faulkner, "Acceptance Speech for Nobel Prize," 1950.

We live in an age in which the human is being constantly diminished, rendered impotent or irrelevant. The forces at work to deprive man of his quality of human–ness are many, and will increase in number and intensity in the decades ahead. A list of such forces need not be exhaustive to be depressing, and in most cases it represents the dark underside of some remarkable human achievement. We have worked feverishly to bring the blessings of the technological society to the entire country, and in the process have poisoned our lands, our water, our air. As the population has exploded and people have crowded into our great cities, the urban areas have become nightmares of hopelessness and despair, degradation and violence. As television and jet transports have contracted and compressed the world, they have subtly diminished man's imaginative conception of himself. As life has become more computerized and homogenized, more comfortable and affluent, its meaning has become more trivial and elusive. Men today live closer together, but exist further apart. They have less cause for labor, but more cause for anguish. They have more of technocracy's abundance and wealth, but they have fewer of nature's simple gifts. They have gained in gewgaws and gadgetry, but they have lost in compassion and humanity.

In Faulkner's view, man will endure because he will continue to talk with his "puny inexhaustible voice." The image is a compelling one. And if, as Faulkner says, man will prevail because he has "a soul, a spirit capable of compassion and sacrifice and endurance," it will be because that soul and that spirit are given reality and made manifest by that "puny inexhaustible voice."

The decline in our community life, our helplessness in finding forms for celebration or leisure, our lack of imaginative power to develop forms to counteract the maladies of our culture—all indicate the extent of man's present disorientation.

It is not difficult to understand how this has come about. The man of today has to bear an enormous and increasing load of intellectual knowledge, while at the same time his emotional world has been steadily atrophying. His emotional apparatus has shrunk to a mere appendage, quite unable to absorb and humanize the knowledge accumulated by his brain. He stands alone.

S. Giedion, "Symbolic Expression in Prehistory and in the First High Civilizations," *Sign, Image, Symbol,* 1966.

The human voice is the bearer of the human spirit. To still it would be, in effect, to still humanity.

It is time now, more than ever before, to sound the note of the human voice in whatever form of language we use. When language itself becomes dehumanized, we have lost the last best hope of the retention of man's human–ness. We must in our language remain stubbornly human if we want to avoid the end of humanity.

The political rhetoric of our time has tended more and more to become dehumanized, to become a series of machine-like slogans hurtled through the streets. "Burn the establishment down" comes from the left. And from the right, the answer: "Love it or leave it." "Kill the pigs," comes back from the left. "Law and order," chants the right. These samples are but a few of the dehumanized phrases that are tossed around the country, and they are indicative of an even deeper disorder that pours forth in the speeches and articles of political prose. Phrases, sentences, and paragraphs appear to be machine-made rather than man-made. They result not from a man thinking and meditating and grappling with the complexities of reality and his view of it—but from someone else's thinking, someone else's vocabulary, someone else's dogmas that have become rigidified and codified and sanctified at the same time that they have become dehumanized and even anti-human.

But politics is only one area of language-use that has tended to become dehumanized. It is easy today to suffocate from or at least choke on the great quantities of organization prose that surround us everywhere in our daily life—in government, in business, in universities, in industry. Some agencies, aware of the lifelessness of prose that has been neutered and machine-tooled, have attempted to restore to it a sense of life by inserting a phony human voice. The result strikes a discordant note not unlike that heard in a voice coming from a computer. The human is there, but it is like a dead or lifeless human. There is an eerie and ghostlike quality about it that chills rather than warms, as the genuinely human voice does. Some business firms have even gone to the trouble of giving their computers human names in order that correspondents will feel that, when they answer the computers' letters, they are writing to human beings.

If scientists elect to study man only by physicochemical methods, they will naturally discover only the physicochemical determinants of his life and find that his body is a machinery of atoms. But they will overlook other human characteristics that are at least as interesting and important. One of them is that man hardly ever reacts passively to external forces. The most characteristic aspect of his behavior is that he responds not only actively but often unexpectedly and creatively. He is the more human the more vigorously he converts passive reactions into creative responses. The mechanical definition of human life misses the point because what is human in man is precisely that which is not mechanical.

René Dubos, *So Human an Animal*, 1968.

In the midst of the contemporary madness, the individual man must plant his feet firmly on his spot of earth and speak forth in his individual voice with all the humanity he can summon. And he must, if he would preserve the human in human life, speak in his own language and nobody else's—and certainly not in the language that is ground out by some machine, or that is used as the officialese of an organization or establishment. He who speaks in another's voice diminishes not only himself but all mankind.

If we are to reconstitute and renew a human dialogue, we must learn to understand one another's voices. This means that no one dialect can be established to the exclusion of others. We need to tune our ears to different accents, different vocabularies, different patterns and intonations. For a long time there was a myth

> Man is a rebel. He is committed
> by his biology not to conform,
> and herein lies the paramount
> reason for the awful tension he
> experiences today in relation to
> Society. . . .
>
> Norman Mailer, *Advertisements*
> *for Myself,* 1959.

perpetuated of a "standard language" in America, deviations from which placed the culprit or guilty party in the lower social reaches —as well as in the lower professional and economic groups. Gradually we have come to understand that a southern drawl or a New England nasalization, a Western twang or a Brooklyn clipped speech are not deviations from some God-appointed norm. And along with this understanding has come the realization that colorful variations in usage, in structural patterns, in word choice are not signs of ignorance and inferiority but signs of healthy language growth and variety. We have come, in short, to know that language is too vital to the individual and the culture, and plays too important a role in exploration, discovery, and identity —both for the self and the culture—to be left to trivial matters of accent, usage, or questions of so-called good grammar.

But as we have learned that language may vary in delightful and interesting ways from area to area, so too must we come to accept the change of language from age to age. We all realize the changes that have come in the English language since the time of Chaucer (fourteenth century), and the time of Shakespeare (sixteenth century), and even the time of Dickens (nineteenth century). But it is easy to overlook the changes of the language that have come in the last two decades. First the beat generation, then the hippies, have brought into being a youth culture that has diligently cultivated its own language—the hip talk that squares cannot understand. But much of this language (and this is always how language grows and changes) has filtered out into general use, including such words as "rap" (discussion), "hip" (knowledgeable), and many more. But aside from the youth culture, radical and rapid changes in our technology and culture have brought about radical and rapid changes in our language. We must, of course, use the language that is in us, the language that comes naturally to us, and there is no need to rush out into the streets to learn the latest words. But we must not suffer under the illusion that ours is the only language permissible and attempt to ignore or stamp out anything new. If a dialogue between generations is to continue, adjustments will need to be made to each other's languages—just as adjustments are made for geographical and other differences. The time is past when one dialect could demand that all others conform to it.

But though language may change, its functions and possibilities —human functions and human possibilities—endure. Through language we come to know ourselves and express ourselves as

> **The individual is the only reality. The further we move away from the individual toward abstract ideas about Homo sapiens, the more likely we are to fall into error. In these times of social upheaval and rapid change, it is desirable to know much more than we do about the individual human being, for so much depends upon his mental and moral qualities.**
>
> Carl G. Jung, "Approaching the Unconscious," *Man and His Symbols,* 1964 (post.).

human beings. Through language we explore, create, transform the structures of society and civilization that give meaning and purpose to our lives as human beings. Through language we relate to the other humans around us, in our family, our locality, our country, the world. If, as Carl Jung says, "The individual is the only reality," it is through language that the individual creates and knows his reality, and it is the human voice that projects that reality into the void. Perhaps our most precious possession and human legacy is the individual voice, but it is up to us to cultivate that voice, and to make it heard in what we say and what we write.

Ideas and Experiments

1. Find some samples of political rhetoric that strike you as dehumanized language. Scan the newspapers for statements or speeches. Analyze them to discover why they strike you this way.

2. Examine the memoranda or letters or announcements of some organization with which you are connected—school, church, business—and find samples of the prose used and analyze its nature—dehumanized, phony human, or genuinely human.

3. Test some of the language that comes naturally to you on your own parents or grandparents, and find what strikes them as strange. Write an account of the experience.

4. Make a collection of words that seem new to you, words brought into the vocabulary because of technological or other development or change. Trace them in the dictionaries as far as you can. Did you discover words not yet in the dictionary? Define them.

5. When you read your own writing, can you hear your own voice? Try your prose out on a friend. What does he find that is distinctively yours in it? Write a character sketch of yourself based on a reading of your writing.

　　　　　　　　VI. THE INDIVIDUAL VOICE

Further Points of Departure

Loren Eiseley, a distinguished contemporary anthropologist, wrote the following parable in "How Human is Man?" included in his book, *The Firmament of Time* (1960):

There is a story about one of our great atomic physicists—a story for whose authenticity I cannot vouch, and therefore I will not mention his name. I hope, however, with all my heart that it is true. If it is not, then it ought to be, for it illustrates well what I mean by a growing self-awareness, a sense of responsibility about the universe.

This man, one of the chief architects of the atomic bomb, so the story runs, was out wandering in the woods one day with a friend when he came upon a small tortoise. Overcome with pleasurable excitement, he took up the tortoise and started home, thinking to surprise his children with it. After a few steps he paused and surveyed the tortoise doubtfully.

"What's the matter?" asked his friend.

Without responding, the great scientist slowly retraced his steps as precisely as possible, and gently set the turtle down upon the exact spot from which he had taken him up.

Then he turned solemnly to his friend. "It just struck me," he said, "that perhaps, for one man, I have tampered enough with the universe." He turned, and left the turtle to wander on its way.

The man who made that remark was one of the best of the modern men, and what he had devised had gone down into the whirlpool. "I have tampered enough," he said. It was not a denial of science. It was a final recognition that science is not enough for man. It is not the road back to the waiting Garden, for that road lies through the heart of man. Only when man has recognized this fact will science become what it was for Bacon, something to speak of as "touching upon Hope." Only then will man be truly human.[13]

1. What are some of the signs of the presence of the personal voice?

2. How would you characterize the style in relation to what appears to be the purpose?

3. The writer is a scientist clearly intent on preserving the "truly human." What evidence in his style is there of a preservation of the human?

4. Can you recall some small incident in your own experience —or the story of some incident—that might serve symbolically in the way this anecdote serves Eiseley?

13. Loren Eiseley, "How Human is Man?" *The Firmament of Time* (New York: Atheneum Publishers, 1960), pp. 148–49.

BIBLIOGRAPHY

This bibliography cites all the sources for the quotations used as epigraphs or as textual inserts throughout the book (for quotations that are a part of the flow of the text itself or that are used in the exercises, see footnotes). After giving essential bibliographical information in each entry, I have indicated the location of the quotation in the text by citing, after page references and in parentheses, the appropriate chapter and section numbers of *Word, Self, Reality.* Thus, (V, 3) means that Chapter V, Section 3, contains the quotation. Where the same book has been used as the source for a number of quotations, I have simply listed them all, along with their locations in my text, at the end of the entry.

"Brihadaranyaka Upanishad," *The Teachings of the Mystics,* ed. Walter T. Stace (New York: Mentor–New American Library, 1960), pp. 36–37 (IV,4).

Brown, Norman O., "Apocalypse: the Place of Mystery in the Life of the Mind," *Harper's Magazine,* May 1961, p. 48 (Intro.); p. 47 (II,2); p. 49 (III, 2 & 3).

Capote, Truman, *Writers at Work: The Paris Review Interviews,* ed. Malcolm Cowley (New York: Viking, 1958), p. 296 (VI,1).

Carnap, Rudolph, *Introduction to Symbolic Logic* (New York: Dover Publications, 1958), p. 2 (II,3).

Carroll, Lewis, *Through the Looking-Glass* (1872; rpt. New York: Random House, 1946), p. 94 (III,4).

Cassirer, Ernst, *An Essay on Man* (New Haven: Yale University Press, 1944), pp. 132–33 (V,1).

Cassirer, Ernst, *Language and Myth,* trans. Susanne K. Langer (New York: Harper, 1946; rpt. New York: Dover Publications, n.d.), p. 61 (IV,1).

Chomsky, Noam, *Cartesian Linguistics* (New York: Harper & Row, 1966), p. 29 (I,4).

Chomsky, Noam, "Linguistics and Politics–Interview," *New Left Review* (Sept.–Oct., 1969), p. 31 (IV,1).

Cohen, Leonard, "Suzanne," 1966. © Project Seven Music, a division of C. T. M. P. (I,3).

Current Research on Dreams, Public Health Service Publication No. 1389 (Washington, D.C.: U.S. Government Printing Office, n.d.), p. 96 (IV,3).

Dubos, René, *So Human an Animal* (New York: Charles Scribner's Sons, 1968), pp. 146–47 (VI,4).

Eliot, T. S., "Sweeney Agonistes," *The Complete Poems and Plays* (New York: Harcourt Brace Jovanovich, 1952), p. 84 (I, 3).

Emerson, Ralph Waldo, "Self-Reliance," *Selections from Ralph Waldo Emerson,* ed. Stephen E. Whicher (Boston: Houghton Mifflin Co., 1957), p. 156 (IV,4).

Faulkner, William, "Acceptance Speech for Nobel Prize," *Essays, Speeches and Public Letters,* ed. James B. Meriwether (New York: Random House, 1965), p. 120 (VI,4).

Faulkner, William, *Faulkner at West Point,* ed. Joseph L. Fant and Robert Ashley (New York: Random House, 1964), pp. 95–96 (VI,3).

Gibson, Walker, "A Note on Style and the Limits of Language," *The Limits of Language,* ed. Walker Gibson (New York: Hill & Wang, 1962), p. 104 (VI,2).

Giedion, S., "Symbolic Expression in Prehistory and in the First High Civilizations," *Sign, Image, Symbol,* ed. Gyorgy Kepes (New York: George Braziller, 1966), p. 79 (II,3); p. 78 (VI,4).

Hansberry, Lorraine, *To Be Young, Gifted and Black,* adapted by Robert Nemiroff (Englewood Cliffs, N.J.: Prentice-Hall, 1969), p. 17 (IV,2); p. 217 (V,3).

Hemingway, Ernest, *Death in the Afternoon* (New York: Charles Scribner's Sons, 1932), p. 2 (IV,2).

Hemingway, Ernest, *Writers at Work: The Paris Review Interviews,* ed. Van Wyck Brooks (New York: Viking, 1963), p. 235 (VI,3).

Hesse, Hermann, *Demian: The Story of Emil Sinclair's Youth,* Intro. Thomas Mann, trans. Michael Roloff and Michael Lebeck (New York: Harper & Row, 1965; rpt. New York: Bantam Books, 1966), p. 108 (IV,1); p. 4 (IV,2).

Hesse, Hermann, *Siddhartha,* trans. Hilda Rosner (New York: New Directions, 1951), pp. 37–38 (V,1).

James, Henry, *The Question of Our Speech* (Boston: Houghton Mifflin Co., 1905), p. 10(V,2).

James, William, *A Pluralistic Universe* (New York: Longmans, Green, & Co., 1909), pp. 212–13 (II,3).

James, William, "Reflex Action and Theism," *The Will to Believe* (New York: Longmans, Green, & Co., 1897), p. 118 (I,3); pp. 118–19 (I,4).

James, William, *The Varieties of Religious Experience* (1902; rpt. New York: Dolphin-Doubleday, n.d.), pp. 213–15 (I,2).

Jespersen, Otto, *Language: Its Nature, Development and Origin* (1922; rpt. New York: W. W. Norton & Co., 1964), p. 434 (III,3).

Jones, LeRoi, "Expressive Language," *Home: Social Essays* (New York: William Morrow & Co., 1966), p. 168 (V,2).

Jones, LeRoi, "LeRoi Jones Talking," *Home: Social Essays* (New York: William Morrow & Co., 1966), p. 182 (II,1).

Jung, Carl G., "Approaching the Unconscious," *Man and His Symbols* (London: Aldus Press, 1964; rpt. New York: Dell Publishing Co., 1968), p. 25 (II,4); pp. 27–28 (III,1); pp. 27–29 (III,2); pp. 34–37 (IV,3); p. 23 (VI,2); and p. 45 (VI,4).

Kluckholn, Clyde, "The Gift of Tongues," *Mirror for Man* (New York: McGraw-Hill Book Co., Inc., 1949), pp. 146–47 (I,1).

Laing, R. D., *The Politics of Experience* (New York: Pantheon, 1967; rpt. New York: Ballantine Books, 1968), pp. 54–55 (I,2); pp. 43–44 (III,2); p. 26 (IV,3); and pp. 126–27 (IV,4).

Langer, Susanne K., *Philosophy in a New Key* (Cambridge, Mass.: Harvard University Press, 1951; rpt. New York: Mentor Books– New American Library, 1961), p. 82 (II,2), p. 113 (V,1).

Lennon, John, "Strawberry Fields Forever," 1967. © Maclen Music Inc., New York (IV,2).

McLuhan, Marshall, *Understanding Media: The Extensions of Man* (New York: McGraw-Hill Book Co., 1964), pp. 3–4,7 (V,3).

Mailer, Norman, *Advertisements for Myself* (New York: G. P. Putnam's Sons, 1959), p. 304 (V,4); p. 305 (VI,4).

Maslow, Abraham H., "Isomorphic Interrelationships Between Knower and Known," *Sign, Image, Symbol,* ed. Gyorgy Kepes (New York: George Braziller, 1966), p. 139 (Intro. & III,3).

Mead, Margaret, *Culture and Commitment: A Study of the Generation Gap* (New York: Natural History Press/Doubleday & Co., Inc., 1970), pp. 62–63, 93–94 (V,4).

Mencken, H. L., "On Style," *A Mencken Chrestomathy* (New York: Alfred A. Knopf, 1949), p. 460 (VI,1).

Mumford, Lewis, "Reflections: Science and Technology III," *The New Yorker,* Oct. 24, 1970, p. 58 (VI, 4).

O'Connor, Flannery, *Mystery and Manners:* Occasional Prose, ed. Robert and Sally Fitzgerald (New York: Farrar, Straus & Giroux, 1969; rpt. New York: The Noonday Press, 1970), pp. 67–68 (V,1).

O'Connor, Frank, *Writers at Work: The Paris Review Interviews* (New York: Viking, 1958), p. 169 (I,4).

Ong, Walter J., "Crisis and Understanding in the Humanities," *Daedalus,* XCVIII (Summer, 1969), 634 (V,3).

Oppenheimer, J. Robert, *The Open Mind* (New York: Simon & Schuster, 1955), p. 54 (VI,1).

Piaget, Jean, *The Language and Thought of the Child* (1930; rpt. New York: Meridian-World, 1955), p. 26 (I,1).

Sapir, Edward, "Language," (1933; rpt. in *Culture, Language and Personality: Selected Essays,* Berkeley: University of California Press, 1964), p. 15 (I,1); pp. 8–9 (I,3).

Simenon, Georges, *Writers at Work: The Paris Review Interviews,* ed. Malcolm Cowley (New York: Viking, 1958), pp. 146–47 (IV,1).

Simon, Paul, "The Sound of Silence," 1964. © Charing Cross Music, New York (I,1).

Sontag, Susan, "One Culture and the New Sensibility," *Against Interpretation* (New York: Farrar, Straus & Giroux, 1966; rpt. New York: Delta–Dell, n.d.), p. 301 (I,4).

Stekel, Wilhelm, quoted in J. D. Salinger, *The Catcher in the Rye* (Boston: Little, Brown, 1951; rpt. New York: Bantam Books, 1964), p. 188 (V,4).

Stevens, Wallace, "Imagination as Value," *The Necessary Angel* (New York: Random House [Vintage 278], 1951). pp. 136, 144, 150, 153, 154 (Intro.).

Styron, William, *Writers at Work: The Paris Review Interviews* (New York: Viking, 1958), p. 276 (II,1).

Suzuki, D. T. *Essays in Zen Buddhism: First Series* (1949; rpt. New York: Grove Press, Inc., 1961). p. 299 (II,4); p. 13 (IV,4).

Thomas, Piri, *Down These Mean Streets* (New York: Alfred A. Knopf, Inc., 1967), p. 10 (IV,1).

Townshend, Peter, "My Generation," 1965. © Devon Music, Inc., New York (V,4).

Vonnegut, Kurt Jr., *Player Piano* (Holt, Rinehart & Winston, 1952), p. 140 (V,4).

Vonnegut, Kurt Jr., *Slaughterhouse Five or the Children's Crusade* (New York: Delacorte Press, 1969), p. 87 (V,4).

Vygotsky, L. S., *Thought and Language* (Cambridge, Mass.: The M.I.T. Press, 1962), pp. 125, 126, 150, 153 (II,1) and p. 150 (II,2).

Whitehead, Alfred North, *Modes of Thought* (New York: The Macmillan Co., 1938; rpt. New York: Capricorn Books, 1958), p. 49 (II,1); p. 57 (IV,1); pp. 49–50 (V,2).

Whitman, Walt, "Song of Myself," *Complete Poetry and Selected Prose,* ed. James E. Miller, Jr. (Boston: Houghton Mifflin Co., 1959), p. 38 (V,2).

Williams, William Carlos, "How to Write," *New Directions in Prose and Poetry,* ed. James Laughlin (New York: New Directions, 1936) p. 45; rpt. in Linda Welshimer Wagner, *The Poems of William Carlos Williams* (Middletown, Conn.: Wesleyan University Press, 1964), pp. 145, 146 (II,4); p. 145 (VI,2).

Williams, William Carlos, *Selected Letters,* ed. John C. Thirlwall (New York: McDowell, Obolensky, 1957), p. 202 (Intro.).

Wittgenstein, Ludwig, *Philosophical Investigations,* trans. G. E. M. Anscombe (New York: The Macmillan Co., 1953), pp. 20–21 (III,1); p. 39 (III,3).

Wittgenstein, Ludwig, *Tractatus Logico-Philosophicus,* trans. D. F. Pears and B. F. McGuiness (1921; rpt. New York: The Humanities Press, 1961), p. 151 (III,1); p. 149 (V,1).

Woolf, Virginia, *The Second Common Reader* (New York: Harcourt Brace Jovanovich, Inc., 1932), pp. 235–236 (V,2).

INDEX TO QUOTATIONS

Ong, Walter J., 169
Oppenheimer, J. Robert, 183

Piaget, Jean, 11
Pound, Ezra, 83

Quinton, A. M., 75, 76

Roszak, Theodore, 181–182

Salinger, J. D., 49, 117, 171
Sapir, Edward, 15, 25
Seishi, Yamaguchi, 152
Shūson, Katō, 152
Simenon, Georges, 115
Simon, Paul, 11
Sontag, Susan, 36
Stein, Gertrude, 199–200
Stekel, Wilhelm, 171
Stevens, Wallace, 1, 5
Styron, William, 45
Suzuki, D. T., 63, 142

Thomas, Piri, 114
Thoreau, Henry David, 80, 141–142, 186, 207
Townshend, Peter, 178

"Upanishad," 138

Vaughan, Henry, 130
Vonnegut, Kurt, Jr., 174, 180
Vygotsky, L .S., 42, 54

Whitehead, Alfred North, 44, 109, 111, 160
Whitman, Walt, 27–28, 71, 91, 119, 139, 148–149, 158, 195–196
Williams, William Carlos, 7, 37, 67, 193
Wittgenstein, Ludwig, 73, 75, 76, 92, 147
Woolf, Virginia, 21–22, 156, 162

"Zen," 49, 69, 140–141